THE TASTE OF OLD HONG KONG

Recipes and memories

from 30 years on the China Coast

THE TASTE OF OLD HONG KONG

Recipes and memories

from 30 years on the China Coast

Fred Schneiter

BLACKSMITH BOOKS

THE TASTE OF OLD HONG KONG

ISBN 978-988-16139-0-5 (paperback)
© 2014 Fred Schneiter
All photographs © 2014 Fred Schneiter except
Sea Dragon under sail, courtesy Lilly Library, and 19th C line art, public domain

Published by Blacksmith Books
5th Floor, 24 Hollywood Road, Central, Hong Kong
www.blacksmithbooks.com

Typeset in Adobe Garamond by Alan Sargent
Printed in Hong Kong

First printing August 2014

"If you've 'eard the East a-callin', you won't never 'eed naught else."
    No! you won't 'eed nothin' else
    But them spicy garlic smells,
    An' the sunshine an' the palm-trees an' the tinkly temple-bells;
    On the road to Mandalay . . .

—*Mandalay*, Rudyard Kipling

Contents

To my family and friends and all the innocent bystanders, who through no fault of their own played an important part in the evolution of this adventure, and especially to the Lovely Charlene—wife, sweetheart, inspiration and unflinching advocate of the proposition that a man should do as he pleases. . . . in the kitchen.

Preface

It was a stroke of particularly good fortune to begin a 30-year career in Asia in the early 1960s, a time when much of the Far East retained the look, feel, charm, and sounds of a century before. It wasn't simply another job in another place but rather a memorable romp through an earlier romantic age.

Today, unceremoniously swept under the rug of change by the twin deities of profit and progress, that Asia now exists only in memory and faded photos. Adaptable and vibrant, Hong Kong remains—and probably always will be—one of the world's most exciting and fascinating cities. But the charming crooked little lanes with bougainvillea cascading from Victorian balconies above the clatter of rickshaws have pretty much vanished, giving way to the impersonal clusters of high-rise apartments and gleaming skyscrapers. But we didn't lose it all. The tantalizing international cuisines and spicy cook pot scents of that earlier time remain.

That's what this little offering is about. Reminiscences of 30 years in the China Seas, along with recipes of memorable old international and regional dishes you could find today in local or foreign households, fancy restaurants or back lanes in Hong Kong; that classy proud old gal who will forever reign as the Queen of Cuisine for those lucky enough to have shared with her some of those grand old yesterdays.

If you've ever daydreamed about what it might be like to drop back into an earlier, less hurried time in an exotic corner of the world, this is how we found the food, the friends and the fun in Old Hong Kong.

Acknowledgments

When I was about six my cousin Ronald taught me that a recipe could be a key to paradise. Three years older, Ronald had attained a level of intuition and a wisdom at which I could only marvel. With just the two of us at home one afternoon he led me into his mother's kitchen, opened a recipe book and the cupboard and in a few magical moments had whipped up for us a whole bowl of chocolate cake icing. I'd never seen anything like it before in my life. A few licks of mother's leftover cake icing was all I'd come to expect. Finishing off the entire bowl was out of the question so the ever-resourceful Ronald called in his faithful dog to destroy the evidence.

Ronald's revelation was like lighting a candle in a darkened library. School assignments were now taken more seriously, with the realization that if you can read you can learn to do anything. On reaching my early teens, having figured out what the Chinese have long known—that good cooks always eat well—I responded with enthusiasm when my mother shared the nuances of grocery shopping and the rudiments of cooking. Years later, I realized I also was learning the important life lessons of planning ahead and following directions. It was in the savory-scented kitchen of my Swiss-born Granny Schneiter that my appreciation of trying something new was nurtured. Tasty Old Country favorites like tongue sandwiches and dandelion salad.

Were it not for them I might think spaghetti grows on trees, comes only in cans and that *"chow yuk"* is what Cantonese say when the *moo goo gai pan* falls below expectations.

Family members and friends the world over were major players in the happy times, offering encouragement, help, recipes, sampling and good counsel.

Among these to whom I am indebted for their valuable inputs and enthusiasm which helped keep my Muse from nodding off—who are not mentioned in the text—include Bob Bratland, Roger and Betsy Davis, Annabel Jackson, Don Kirk, Wayne Kingsley, Dennis and Mary Leventhal, Kian Tiong and Magdalene Lie, K.H. Lu, Willie Mark, Fleur Chanco Noeth, Tim and Mei Oviatt, Sunun Setboonsarng, Peter Suter, Claudia Tam, Gene and Linda Vickers, Wah and Vivian Wong, Yeul Byong Yoon, Madam Zhuli, Lisa Nead, Shu Hua Roland and Candy Tong.

Thanks also to Jan Clark, Tom and Michael Lie, Bob McQuown and Lonnie Watne, whose *savoir-faire* at the computer carried me across the finish line. And in the process, saved my computer from being sold to a small-boat owner, as an anchor.

And, of course, thanks to publisher Pete Spurrier and editor Alan Sargent whose combined editorial alchemy transformed 30 years of China Seas adventures into something you might like to have on your nightstand, bookshelf or in the kitchen.

Chef's Notes

Techniques, ingredients and other nuggets of information that apply to more than one recipe.

Spelling
The spelling of Chinese words in this book is eclectic, using the most familiar version, whether Wade-Giles, Pinyin or other Romanization. No political or cultural bias is implied!

Weights and Measures
The recipes use common American cooking units. Metric equivalents are below.

1 teaspoon	5 cc
1 tablespoon	15 cc
1 cup	240 cc
1 ounce	28 g
1 pound	450 g

If buying food in Asia, metric units are common, but traditional units are still used. These vary from country to country. In Hong Kong markets you may buy food by the "Chinese pound" aka "catty" aka *kan*: 610 g, which is divided into 16 "Chinese ounces" aka "tael" aka *leung*: 38 g.

Servings

Chinese recipes do not lend themselves to a set number of servings. In the traditional family style the number of servings from one dish depends on the number of diners and the number and size of the dishes. The more diners, the greater variety of food. When guests are involved there will be even more dishes and they will be more fancy. The amount of rice on the table depends on how many other dishes are served. It is customary to always have some rice on the table. Westerners in a Chinese restaurant, unfamiliar with the system, typically order a dish all to themselves, so you will see one devouring a big mound of fried noodles while his or her companion takes on a platter of shrimp. A Chinese couple would share the noodles and shrimp, along with perhaps a chicken dish and a couple of appetizers. In view of such considerations, the serving sizes indicated for many of the following Chinese recipes should be considered as rough approximations.

Woks and Steamers

In using a wok, you have two styles to choose from: the round-bottom traditional Chinese wok or the flat-bottom one, designed for use on Western stoves. Or you may use a large heavy Western frying pan with high sides. I have always used two woks. A good carbon steel one and a cheaper stainless steel one which is reserved for steaming, thus protecting the patina which has evolved from the frying. You'll find woks and bamboo steamers in Asian markets or well-stocked kitchen shops. You may also find a steel collar or ring to hold a round-bottom wok steady on a Western stovetop. Be advised, these collars, and a large Western frying pan may damage some types of stove tops.

We steam food in one of those lidded, multi-tiered bamboo steamer baskets which are found in Asian food stores and specialty kitchen shops. Available in a variety of sizes, they are well suited to hold a main course, an appetizer, a couple fancy dumplings or a few shrimp. The bamboo lid prevents steam from condensing and dribbling back onto the food, which can happen with a metal lid. Break in a new bamboo steamer by steaming it, empty, over boiling water for a few minutes or by a good rinse in hot running water.

Place some cabbage or lettuce leaves, or a piece of white cotton material on the bamboo slats inside the steamer and set the food on that. When lifting the lid hold it so it deflects the hot steam away from you.

Get the water level close enough to the bottom of the bamboo steamer so the food gets plenty of steam, but not so close that boiling water can splash into the dish. Keep a pot of hot water on the stove to top up the boiling water if needed.

While you can steam food in one of those expanding metal baskets with interleaved perforated panels (which open like a blooming flower bud) you may instead improvise and use a trivet or a bowl in a large pot to hold food above the boiling water, or the steamer may be set on wooden chopsticks or skewers.

Sugar, Salt, Spices and Flavorings
When "sugar" is listed as an ingredient, amber-colored raw turbinado sugar which you should find at the supermarket in crystal form, is recommended. This is similar to what the Chinese use and call "rock sugar" or "rock candy." For "salt," kosher salt is recommended. For "pepper," freshly-ground is preferable.

Some unaccustomed to coriander find the herb's taste "soapy." A problem easily resolved if you simply place the just-rinsed and chopped coriander on the table in a separate bowl so diners may serve themselves if they wish.

Shao Xing rice wine (pronounced "shao shing"), will be found at a well-stocked Asian market. Warmed, it is served as a dinner wine in a cordial glass or sake cup. If you find it labeled "cooking wine" it has had one and a half percent salt added so keep that in mind when adding salt to a recipe. Unsalted Shao Xing is well worth the search. A good dry sherry may be substituted if necessary.

Dark soy sauce is more outspoken than the regular soy sauce which Westerners are accustomed to. Regular soy sauce, the type generally found in Western markets, is considered light soy sauce and appears that way in some recipes. Then there is a low-sodium variety which is labeled "lite."

Something Different

Living in one of the world's major tourist destinations, the culinary epicenter of the China Seas and a world-class capital of fine dining, prompts many Hong Kong insiders to choose their restaurants following the ancient axiom "the fewer tourists the better the food."

Fortunately, if you know your way around, the choices are virtually unlimited with a dazzling diversity of restaurants offering every imaginable ethnic favorite from arroz con pollo to zabaglione. Our destination of choice on evenings we felt like having something different was the Causeway Bay typhoon shelter, known to some as "the tycoon shelter" as it harbored the sleek and costly craft of the Royal Hong Kong Yacht Club. It also afforded moorage for a small flotilla of durable seaworthy family junks.

The only tourists in evidence on these outings were those who'd been smuggled in by locals, quite likely with the visitors' absolute assurance they wouldn't reveal the location to anyone else. The inclination toward secrecy was perhaps overblown. Even having heard about the place a stranger had little chance of getting to it without help.

Logistically, with its access blocked by sea walls, the harbor and the life-threatening speedway of Victoria Park Road, there were only two reasonable approaches. One was the little-known underground passageway which carried utility services under the road from the basement of the Excelsior Hotel. The other was the harrowing approach by cab from the west. This entailed somehow getting the driver to understand that he had to pull off the speedway *right here* to discharge passengers in the blink of an eye. If you failed to stop exactly on target the cab would hurtle up the overpass onto Gloucester Road, whisking you off in the other direction.

Tricky. And that's not all. It was essential to have a Cantonese-speaker make a phone call to reserve a junk which would comfortably accommodate a half dozen or so people. Once aboard, the little craft wheezed and bobbed out to the center of the shelter into a tiny fleet of junks and sampans rolling at anchor on the inky night sea. Each cast a glow from a bare bulb or two. Some were garlanded with multi-colored Christmas tree lights which sparkled and skittered across the choppy waves. As our anchor dropped, small junks pulled alongside like moths to a flame. One was the brightly-lit booze boat, loaded to the gunnels with hard liquor, beer, soft drinks, fruit, snacks and cigarettes. The music boat had a jovial three-piece off-key percussion band with a vocalist who belted out a cacophony of old-time songs in Chinglish. One of the more profitable businesses on the water, a generous tip assured an early upping of their anchor.

Then there were the sampans. Barely a dozen feet long, these were powered by a single oar which extended straight back from the stern. The vessel takes its name from the fact it is little more than three boards (*saam paan*) nailed together. Most typhoon shelter sampans were miniature floating kitchens.

That's how we met Suki who churned alongside offering a variety of stir-fried seafood. His specialty—a favorite of typhoon shelter regulars—was clams. After we got to know Suki he shared the recipe. I tucked it away and didn't get to it for quite some time, confident that when I did it would, typically, take considerable experimentation to figure out what key ingredient Suki had "forgotten" to include. When I finally tried the recipe I was amazed to have it turn out exactly the way he does it, causing the Lovely Charlene to note after dinner, "Suki's clams even smell great when the dishes are being washed." It's a rare restaurateur who will share a recipe, much less a house specialty. Or, in Suki's case, a boat specialty.

Of course Suki had to be confident in the knowledge a Westerner couldn't go into competition with him as it's highly unlikely that one could ever figure out how to propel a sampan with that single off-the-stern oar, without simply going around in circles or falling overboard.

If you aren't yet into stir-frying, get yourself a wok and give this great dish a try. . . .

SUKI'S CLAMS
serves 2 to 4

Sauce

1 tablespoon black bean and garlic sauce

8 slices fresh ginger, peeled, ¼ inch thick, lightly chopped

1 teaspoon crushed red pepper flakes

1 tablespoon sugar

2 teaspoons salt

2 tablespoons regular soy sauce

Ingredients

2 pounds of steamers or littleneck clams, rinsed, in the shell

3 tablespoons peanut oil for frying

Accompaniment

1 loaf French bread, sliced, for dipping

Mix together in a small bowl the bean and garlic sauce, ginger, pepper flakes, sugar, salt and soy sauce. Warm wok over medium high heat about 2 minutes until a drop of water falling onto it makes just one sizzling bounce. Add oil and increase heat to high and in about 1 minute when oil begins to shimmer and light haze (not smoke) begins to rise add sauce from the bowl. Stir-fry just 2 or 3 seconds. Add clams and stir-fry over high heat I minute. Cover and reduce heat for I minute. Remove cover, and stir occasionally a few minutes more until clams open. Place clams in serving bowl with juice and serve at once, with plenty of French bread for dipping into the juice while the clams are eaten.

Tips—Black bean and garlic sauce will be found at an Asian market or at your supermarket's Asian section. Overcooking toughens clams. Discard any clams with broken shells or which float or which will not close tightly during rinsing under cold running water. When dining discard any which are not well opened. The American West Coast hard shell Manila and steamer clams are similar to those used by Suki but any small meaty clams should work fine. Commercially raised clams from the supermarket generally need only to be rinsed and drained. Eat them individually by hand, extracting the meat with chopsticks. Dip the French bread into the juice. It's finger food, so feel free to approach this business casually. Set a big bowl on the table for empty shells and provide each diner with a damp, chilled washcloth. A bowl of warm black tea with a few thin slices of lemon may also be provided to rinse fingers after eating. A final word of caution. Under no circumstance use your best tablecloth. In the typhoon shelter the table covering was either newspapers or butcher paper, which made sense. And would have tasted pretty good if you were set adrift for any length of time and had nothing else to eat.

The Fear of Trying

Webster's defines "phobia" as a fear of "irrational and excessive" proportions, and that pretty well describes what newcomers often exhibit in initial skirmishes with banqueting in China. Chinese hosts are aware of this odd foreign disinclination toward good food and their menu selections take this into account when foreigners are at the table.

My old friend Jiang Xi, President of the China Cuisine Association, takes a different approach and I have often seen him, even in the Great Hall of the People, nudge a nervous foreign guest as a particularly outstanding pork or chicken dish is brought to the table and say, with a casual nod and twinkle in his eye, "Dog. You like dog?"

One of my favorite fear-of-trying reminiscences occurred during lunch in Hong Kong with an American businessman who was on his first visit to Asia. For dessert I'd ordered an almost-translucent cold, green soup. As the soup with its rich luster like an outstanding piece of jade was placed before us I remarked casually, "Green fisheye soup. Wonderful."

On our way back to the office the visitor remarked somewhat in awe, "I don't know how you could eat that."

"What?"

"That fisheye soup."

"Holy smoke! I was so engrossed with mine I didn't notice you hadn't eaten yours. That was chilled, honeydew melon, laced with coconut milk, sugar and tapioca. Absolute ambrosia. We just call it fisheye soup because of those tapioca pearls."

This outstanding dish is not typically Chinese and the honeydew melon is not native to China. The seeds were presented to the Chinese in 1945 during a visit by US Vice President Henry Wallace, a former Secretary of Agriculture and the honeydew is still widely known in China as "Wallace melon." It flourishes in the northwest Silk Road region, where—typical of the fruit there—it is sweeter than the honeydew we have in the West.

If you ever come across a dessert item on a Chinese menu which reads "Green Fisheye Soup" order it without fear, or better still, make it at home. . . .

COLD GREEN MELON SOUP
serves 6

Ingredients
¼ cup small pearl tapioca

1 cup canned coconut milk

3 tablespoons granulated sugar

½ cup cold milk

1 small honeydew melon

Add tapioca to ½ cup water in a small bowl and set aside 45 minutes and then drain off and discard the water. In a medium saucepan add tapioca, coconut milk and sugar and mix well. Heat on low simmer, stirring frequently until mixture begins to thicken, 5 to 10 minutes. Stir in cold milk and set aside. When cooled to room temperature cover with plastic wrap and transfer to refrigerator. Quarter the melon, remove seeds and peel. Cut up melon and mix in blender until it becomes thoroughly liquefied. Fold tapioca, coconut milk, sugar and milk mixture into liquefied melon with wooden spoon until thoroughly blended. Cover with plastic wrap and refrigerate 1 or 2 hours. Stir slightly before serving chilled in (1 cup size) Chinese rice bowls.

Tips—A not-quite-ripe honeydew feels slick to the touch, whereas, if you press your fingertips hard on a ripe one and run them across it, you may feel a very slight sticky resistance. Refrigerated, this soup may be made a day before serving. In that case, stir well just before serving.

Think of Chopsticks as Friends

If unaccustomed to chopsticks you'll find the going easier—in initial encounters—simply by maintaining an affirmative attitude. Dismiss any thought that chopsticks are an ancient form of torture, invented to intimidate and frustrate fumbling foreign fingers. The secret is to relax and to keep in mind that Chinese also drop greasy things on the tablecloth and sometimes even on other people . . . and it isn't a big deal. It happens.

Lunching on Hong Kong's "Food Street" in Causeway Bay, a Cantonese lady beside me, at our tiny shared table, casually chopsticked a pork chop from her bowl of noodle soup.

Taking a dainty nibble, gravity suddenly prevailed. In an instant the chop plopped into her bowl, launching half her soup directly into my lap. The poor young thing was terribly embarrassed despite my assurance that it was OK. These things happen. Even to Chinese.

Then there was the Hong Kong Broccoli Incident which occurred while hosting a delegation of old friends from China's Grain Bureau. Midway through the dinner we were served a steamy platter of slender, leafy, oyster-sauced Chinese broccoli. In the polite gesture of giving face to a dinner companion, the delegation leader, a particularly close family friend, was in the process of putting broccoli on my plate when her smile suddenly vanished as the slippery stuff started to slide off her chopsticks. She tried to catch the little varmint but, misjudging the thrust, catapulted the goopy glob straight into my tie. She managed just one or two tentative little embarrassed giggles before she and the entire table doubled over in gleeful guffaws as the gooey vegetable trailed a slow slimy slalom down the entire length of the tie.

Not only did it demonstrate what a fun food broccoli could be, it illustrated the wisdom of the old proverb, "When working together, laugh together." Had this simply been one of those ubiquitous run-of-the-mill Chinese business dinners, rather than a gathering of old friends, it could have proven a disaster.

Slapstick scenarios aside, this is a tasty and easy dish but if someone tries to put some on your plate, watch out. . . .

CHINESE BROCCOLI IN OYSTER SAUCE
serves 2 to 4
Ingredients
1 pound Chinese broccoli
¼ teaspoon salt
¾ tablespoon peanut oil
Sauce
3 tablespoons Chinese oyster sauce
½ teaspoon sesame oil
½ teaspoon peanut oil
1 teaspoon fresh ginger, peeled and minced

Cut off and discard leggy bottom part of broccoli stalks. Remove and discard any tougher large leaves, leaving intact the more tender smaller ones. Peel lower section of stalks below the leaves. Rinse broccoli well under cold running water. Shake off excess water. In a large pot, bring 3 quarts of water to a rolling boil and add the salt and peanut oil. Meanwhile, in a small saucepan, combine oyster sauce, sesame oil, peanut oil and ginger. Stir a few times, cover and bring to a low simmer for 30 seconds and set sauce aside. Add broccoli to the boiling water and when water returns to a boil, cover and cook 5 to 7 minutes, stirring occasionally. Doneness may be checked by chilling a piece and biting into it. The more fresh and tender the broccoli, the less cooking time is required. Remove broccoli from boiling water while it retains its color and is tender, yet crisp. Drain well for a few minutes in a colander, shaking off and discarding excess liquid. Place broccoli in a large bowl, pour sauce evenly over it and toss gently to mix. Arrange broccoli on serving plate. May be served hot or at room temperature with heated sauce.

Tips—Serving broccoli at room temperature frees you up for other last-minute details at the stove. In this case, set the cooked broccoli aside for up to 3 hours and add the sauce hot just before serving. Western broccoli works quite well, but Chinese broccoli is available in Asian markets and is worth seeking out for its distinctive taste and texture.

The Sea Dragon's *Dinner Party*

The *Sea Dragon* was the most flamboyant and highly heralded junk ever to sail out of Hong Kong. In a bold bid for international acclaim as a major attraction at the San Francisco World's Fair, it lurched into a mid-Pacific storm in early 1939 and vanished on its way to California.

US Navy planes searched 250,000 square miles of open sea west of Midway Island without finding a trace of the vessel or its crew of twelve. Among the missing was the audacious American vagabond and travel writer Richard Halliburton.

It was Halliburton who conceived the idea of building the junk and sailing it to America, where he was convinced "it would be the most exciting concession at the fair." Halliburton was one of the early advocates of the theory that the Chinese might well have discovered the New World before Columbus, who stumbled upon it quite by chance in seeking a sea route to China by sailing west.

In addition to providing material for lectures, magazine and newspaper articles and his next adventure book, Halliburton saw the voyage as something fun and exciting which few would ever have the opportunity to do.

This was the catalyst which had driven him endlessly around the world in the pursuit of high adventure during the two decades before he launched the voyage of the ill-starred *Sea Dragon*.

In an era when few ventured far from home, Halliburton sought out the remote and romantic recesses of the world. He seemed to have been virtually everywhere, answering the call of any adventure which struck his fancy. Wanting to do "everything once" he lived by Tennyson's precept: "For my purpose holds to sail beyond the sunset, until I die. To strive, to seek, to find, and not to yield."

When the writer/wanderer wasn't actively engaged in the pursuit of something exciting it seemed to lie in wait for him. Returning to Hong Kong from a Macau holiday one evening in 1922 he was aboard the *Sui An* when it was seized by sixty howling gun-wielding pirates. He relished the excitement of what he termed, "the most outrageous holdup Hong Kong has known." He just happened to be in Beijing during the last great ostentation of Imperial China, the wedding of Pu Yi, the last emperor.

Hong Kong had long been one of Halliburton's favorite places. He found it "an overpowering sight" and as a boy had felt it to be about as far away as any place could be. The Repulse Bay Hotel—just down the road from our apartment—he considered "without doubt the most splendidly situated and beautiful hotel in Asia."

To prepare for the voyage from Hong Kong to San Francisco's Treasure Island, Halliburton arrived in Hong Kong in late October 1938. The Japanese had just taken Canton (Guangzhou) just across the border. While Hong Kong residents got their minds off the gathering war clouds in Asia and Europe by going to see Walt Disney's *Snow White and the Seven Dwarfs* at the Queen's and Alhambra theaters, Halliburton busied himself with the "perpetual crisis" of building and outfitting a sea-going junk. One day he wrote home that his shipyard workers were striking because he'd failed to give them a party. "Every self-respecting workman in China expects the employer to give two parties per job, one at the beginning, one when the work is finished. And we had given no party at all. We were guilty of the worst possible manners. So perhaps a sit-down strike would teach us the customs of the country."

With fifty men on the job, the interpreter estimated that a whopping big blowout would cost about US$9 for the whole shebang. Cautioned to not give the money to No. 1 wife, as she could be expected to give only a US$6 dinner and keep the difference, Halliburton turned the money over to No. 4 wife, who, he wrote, "was supposed to be less grasping."

The $9 feast amazed the American host. "There were barrels and baskets of Chinese food. The rice wine would almost have floated our *Sea Dragon*. There were girls and music. In no time everyone was tipsy."

Toward dawn, the party-goers snuggled into the ship's unfinished ribs and scaffolding and caught a brief snooze before returning to work with renewed vigor.

We don't have an exact record of what was served that evening, but the party could well have included these popular and easy dishes, with which Halliburton was surely familiar from his travels around the China Seas. . . .

SHRIMP AND GREEN PEAS
serves 2 to 4
Sauce
½ teaspoon Shao Xing wine or good dry sherry
½ egg white, unbeaten
1 teaspoon cornstarch
Ingredients
1 cup small shrimp, cooked and shelled
3 tablespoons peanut oil for frying
1 spring onion, rinsed, with roots and top few inches of green tops trimmed off and discarded, cut into 1-inch pieces
1-inch piece fresh ginger, peeled, cut in half, lightly smashed or heavily scored with a knife
½ teaspoon salt
½ teaspoon sugar
1 cup frozen green garden peas, defrosted on large flat plate 10 minutes

In a medium bowl combine well the wine, egg white and cornstarch. Gently fold in shrimp, coating thoroughly. Warm wok over medium high heat about 2 minutes until a drop of water falling onto it makes just one sizzling bounce. Add oil and increase heat to high and in about 1 minute when oil begins to shimmer and light haze (not smoke) begins to rise add onion and ginger and stir-fry 1 minute to flavor oil and then remove onion and ginger with slotted spoon or wooden chopsticks and discard. Immediately add shrimp to hot oil and stir-fry until evenly heated, just under 30 seconds. Immediately add salt and sugar and gently fold in peas until well mixed and thoroughly heated, just over 15 seconds. Turn out onto serving plate. Serve hot.

Tips—This calls for small peeled, cooked, possibly tinned, shrimp about the size of a small cashew or somewhat smaller and known variously as bay shrimp, salad shrimp and shrimpmeat. If using a larger shrimp or prawn slice to about the size of a small cashew. Be careful not to overcook shrimp as this toughens them.

VELVET CORN AND CRAB SOUP
serves 2 to 4
Ingredients
15-ounce can chicken broth
15-ounce can creamed corn
1 cup cooked Dungeness crab meat
salt and ground white pepper to taste
1 tablespoon cornstarch
1 teaspoon Colman's English dry mustard
2 egg whites, beaten with fork until bubbly

Garnish

1 ½ tablespoon fresh coriander leaves, rinsed and coarsely chopped

In large saucepan, bring chicken broth, corn, crab, salt and pepper to low boil. Add 2 tablespoons of cold water to a small bowl, stir in cornstarch and add to soup. Stir until soup thickens, about 30 seconds. Add mustard to 1 teaspoon of cold water and stir into soup thoroughly. Turn off heat, give egg whites a final brisk whisk with a fork and holding the egg whites a few inches above the surface of the soup, pour them slowly onto the surface in a thin stream in a circular motion in one direction. Stir once. Add garnish. Serve hot.

Tips—White chicken breast may be substituted for the crab. A few drops of regular soy sauce may be added to the surface of the soup immediately before adding coriander. Canned crab may be substituted for fresh cooked crab but the fresh is superior in flavor and texture.

Real Junk Food

Lunching at Singapore's proud old Raffles Hotel in the early 1960s, a British friend remarked that he'd soon be moving to Hong Kong which in those days was—rather like Singapore—a tranquil tropical backwater, much more quaint and cozy than it is today.

"Hong Kong's great," I conceded. "Colorful and charming. But watch out for island fever. At least Singapore isn't isolated. You can drive across the causeway into Malaysia and you can almost toss a coconut into Indonesia. Hong Kong's tiny. The China border is closed and you're cut off from everywhere else by the sea."

"Boating, my boy!" the portly Old Colonial enthused. "Boating! Hong Kong has some of the best in all bloody Asia. That's how I'll spend every unencumbered moment." Swirling the ice in with what remained of his midday gin and tonic he grinned and intoned with a flourish, " 'I must go down to the seas again, for the call of the running tide is a wild call and a clear call that may not be denied.' John Masefield. British of course."

As I came to know Hong Kong better I learned, to my good fortune through boating friends, the Old Colonial's enthusiasm for pleasure boating there was well-founded. Aside from the beaches, the cinema and trekking Hong Kong's spectacular hiking trails, boating was the enclave's most popular holiday pursuit, with boats of assorted shapes and sizes casting off at every opportunity with the skipper's national flag fluttering brightly in the sea breeze.

The most popular craft in Hong Kong's holiday fleet has long been the sturdy, virtually-unsinkable motorized junk. With a design some 4,000 years old the craft's flat keel rides rough seas as effortlessly as a cork. Averaging some 40 to 60 feet from bow to stern the typical junk is powered by a reliable 80 to 120 horsepower diesel engine.

In her earlier quiet life, up to just a few decades ago, Hong Kong had a huge literally floating population of "boat people" who lived out their lives on such junks and smaller motorized sampans as well. You'd see them anchored in large clusters—rail to rail—in virtually every bay, inlet and typhoon shelter. Children attended school on little covered barges within the floating cities.

Something of an obligatory tourist photo opportunity, the little boats were more fun to photograph than they were to live on. Today, Hong Kong's old floating suburbs have pretty much disappeared, with a higher standard of living enabling former occupants to relocate to high-rise housing estates on land. In many cases, their former floating abodes have been converted to spiffy weekend pleasure craft.

Although it's unlikely many foreigners actually got around to pursue the idea, on almost every holiday outing someone would mention how they would like to have a Hong Kong junk on the lake or bay back home when they retired.

While longer cruises by Hong Kong's pleasure craft were common—some to other countries—the typical holiday outing began shortly after sunrise with owners and guests lugging aboard their coolers, heavily laden with the day's repast. The return generally coincided with sunset, typically after a quiet afternoon at anchor in some remote and comfortable becalmed cove which afforded a cool dip and a stroll along a deserted beach.

Our communal coolers afforded a posh repast. And, unfailingly decimated to the very last nibble were two of the Lovely Charlene's highly-praised contributions to our galley. Her zippy spring onion roll and a sensational crab mousse, the latter adapted from a recipe from *In The Beginning,* the appetizer cookbook of the American Women's Association of Hong Kong.

Widely referred to as "real junk food," our sustenance was always something memorable. . . .

SPRING ONION ROLLS
Ingredients
1 (4½-ounce) jar sliced dried beef, about 26 slices
26 spring onions, rinsed, cut from the white root end into 1½-inch pieces, with roots trimmed off, discarding the roots and green tops
cream cheese, softened

Loosely separate beef slices, place in bowl and give two light hot water rinses to reduce saltiness. Pat dry with paper towel and separate into individual slices and cut in half. Pat onions dry with paper towel. Spread one side of beef slice with cream cheese. Place onion at one end of the beef slice and roll it up so that onion is snugly wrapped in the beef. Ends of the onion will be visible at both ends of the roll. Repeat with each beef and onion slice, laying them carefully in a container. Cover and refrigerate until serving later in the day.

Tips—Simply adjust the number downward, to a dozen or whatever, if you are serving just a few people. Sliced dried beef may be found in a glass jar in the tinned meat section of the supermarket. Rather than discarding the green tops cut from the onions, these may be chopped and used as garnish for other Asian dishes. It's best not to start nibbling on spring onion rolls as you prepare them or you may not have enough for the guests.

CRAB MOUSSE

Ingredients

1 can cream of mushroom soup, undiluted

1 envelope unflavored gelatin

¾ cup mayonnaise

6-ounce package cream cheese, softened

1 cup celery, finely chopped

1 ½ cups cooked Dungeness crab meat

1 small white onion, peeled, grated

Garnish

4 paper-thin lemon slices

4 sprigs fresh watercress or parsley

Accompaniment

crackers or sliced baguettes

Warm soup. Dissolve gelatin in 3 tablespoons of cold water and add to soup. Add mayonnaise, cream cheese, celery, crab and onion. Stir occasionally until cheese becomes smooth. Rinse a mold in cold water and dry thoroughly. Line mold with plastic wrap, add mixture, cover with plastic wrap and refrigerate overnight. Just before serving, remove top plastic wrap, press serving plate tightly over mold and turn upside down onto serving plate. Garnish and serve cold.

Tips—Because of its delicate flavor, this is best spread on bland soda saltine crackers rather than with the more outspoken potato or corn chips. Canned crab may be substituted for fresh cooked crab but fresh cooked crab is always best.

Food for Thought

Semi-snoozing by the hotel pool in Singapore, barely aware of the muted occasional discourse of a nearby Western couple, I perked up on hearing the lady say, "I don't eat Chinese food because of the MSG." My initial impulse was to apologize for overhearing and point out that the flavor-enhancer monosodium glutamate is not an essential part of Chinese cooking, despite the widely held view to the contrary. I considered explaining that I cook Chinese food often and haven't used MSG for decades because not only can a hearty hit of it jolt me awake at 2 a.m. for a two-hour bout with sleeplessness, you can get the full measure of flavor without it, simply by using a bit of salt or proper use of herbs, spices, and marinades. Or by slow simmering, making soup a day ahead of time and using ingredients which most complement one another. You can make a great soup with no salt.

And that applies to many dishes, properly prepared.

That's what I might have said. But it was one of those steamy midyear equatorial days, when the sun is so directly overhead you have to lift your foot to get a good look at your shadow, so I refrained from rising to the defense of Chinese cuisine and drifted into a proper Singapore Sunday snooze. What the heck.

The Chinese Restaurant Syndrome? Sure, some people experience one of a variety of allergic reactions from too generous an offering of MSG. Or perhaps just a tad. And the problem is, bad cooks tend to use it a lot and until recent years Chinese restaurants, both in and out of China, seemed inclined in many cases to fill the kitchen with folks who really should have been in another line of work. But good upscale Chinese restaurants have become common, and realizing some customers avoid MSG, menus and food product labels often now state they are "MSG-Free." Or to be more precise, "No MSG added" as it's a common ingredient in many condiments which are used by restaurants and food processors.

Preparing your own food at home is the best way to avoid the problem. If you're using MSG at home without an allergic reaction to it, good for you. However, before wielding a wok for dinner guests, you might want to ask if they have any thoughts on that.

Avoiding MSG altogether isn't always easy where Asian food is involved. And it is one of the flavor-enhancers widely used in popular processed foods in the West today, where it is likely to appear on the label under a variety of aliases. Today 15 countries produce MSG, with estimates of annual global production at close to 2 million tons a year. So the lady at poolside really had little reason to single out Chinese cuisine as the culprit.

Another widespread misconception about Chinese cooking is that it's time-consuming and difficult. It can be, but there are many excellent dishes which are whipped up with relative ease or which may be simplified. Many of the more popular dishes came out of the countryside where overworked wives, coming in from the field, lacked the luxury of spending all afternoon on a dish as the Emperor's kitchen cadre did daily as a matter of course.

Lily Lee Levin—wife of Ambassador Burton Levin and an authority on what goes on in Chinese kitchens—authored the long overdue book, *Scrutable Chinese Cooking,* dedicated to demystifying and simplifying the cuisine. One evening after dinner at the Levin residence at Hong Kong's Deep Water Bay, Lily noted, "For we Chinese, eating may be the First Happiness but preparation and cooking Chinese food is an integral part of the pleasure." But she'll also tell you to keep things simple in the kitchen and not necessarily follow recipes exactly to the letter. "If you prefer things sweeter, go ahead and use more sugar and it isn't absolutely necessary to boil a chicken all afternoon if you have a can of good chicken broth on hand."

We've attended dinners in Chinese homes in China where the wife, even one with a family cook, spent much of the evening in the kitchen personally attending to her special dishes while the guests were eating. As Lily says, "Cooking should be fun." Following her lead, we no longer spend two days putting together a special Chinese holiday dinner for a few friends as we did during our early years in Taipei. For special occasions we've learned to go for less time consuming dishes, perhaps preparing a few of those a day or so ahead and refrigerating them, while selecting a few main dishes to prepare the day of the dinner. It doesn't have to amount to much more effort than you would have with any other cuisine. Keep it fun and relaxed and remember there is no rule that says you can't pick up one or two favorites at a good Chinese restaurant that afternoon to fill out the menu—perhaps wonton soup or spring rolls—which you can reheat.

Soups may be made a day or so before. Rice is always served and this takes virtually no time, especially with an electric rice cooker. Soybeans in the pod are a fast and delicious appetizer. Look for them (uncooked) in the supermarket freezer section under their Japanese name, *edamame.* These take just a 5 minute rolling boil in water seasoned with some regular soy sauce or a little salt. (Served in the pod you squirt the peas into your mouth with your fingers, discarding the pods.)

If doing stir-fry have guests take their seats as soon as the wok is hot. Stir-fry dishes take only a few moments and to simplify things, serve this as your first main dish and plan no more than one stir-fry dish per meal, to avoid having to pop up and down through the dinner. Scheduling the dinner on a weekend contributes to ease of preparation which—with the color, action, steam and sizzle of Chinese cuisine—helps make it a fun social event, particularly when guests are invited to involve themselves in the chopping and mixing.

Rather than a complicated dessert we often opt for the Taiwanese favorite, oranges sliced into wedges with the skin on. Eaten with the fingers this takes only seconds to slice and arrange on a dish and set aside until time to serve. Fruit affords a typical and easy conclusion to a Chinese dinner. Serve a chilled melon cut into half-inch cubes. Nice. Or a chilled, canned fruit such as mandarin oranges, or litchis. With a little planning, and a few shortcuts, in about an hour, a memorable Chinese dinner can be set before a few guests, or one guest who you'd really like to impress.

Cantonese roast pork, one of the most popular appetizers in China and in Chinese-American restaurants, is a favorite which requires little preparation. It can be made a day or so before and held in the refrigerator. And it keeps well in the freezer. It is served either hot or cold, in ¼ inch slices, and while featured as an appetizer it also appears chopped, in stir-fry dishes and soups. It's great with mustard as a sandwich as well, in the unlikely event you find yourself with leftovers. That rarely happens when it's served as a cold party snack or Chinese appetizer with a side dish dip of white sesame seeds alongside a dish of spicy hot mustard made with Colman's mustard powder.

This roast pork always brings to mind a get-acquainted luncheon with Chinese businessmen in the early 1970s shortly after we'd moved to Taipei from Manila. As we started with this as an appetizer, the host asked if I knew what it was.

"Yes. Cantonese roast pork. This is better than what I make at home. Next time I'll use more *wu shang fen.*"

This illustrates that no matter what seemingly innocuous thing you might learn about how things are done in the Far East, some day it's going to come in handy.

And while it might sound exotic this *was* pretty innocuous because you'll find *wu shang fen* on your supermarket spice shelf labeled with the literal translation "Chinese five spice powder". . . .

CANTONESE ROAST PORK
serves 4 to 6 per tenderloin

Ingredients

1 or 2 lean pork tenderloins, rinsed and patted dry with paper towels

Marinade

½ tablespoon salt

5 tablespoons sugar

2 medium garlic cloves, peeled and finely chopped or passed through a garlic press

2 spring onions, rinsed, with roots and top few inches of green tops trimmed off and discarded, minced

2 tablespoons white vinegar

2 tablespoons Shao Xing wine or good dry sherry

1 teaspoon Chinese five spice powder

1½ teaspoons red food coloring

Accompaniment

3 tablespoons white sesame seeds

Colman's mustard powder, mixed with water to desired consistency in an amount roughly equal to the amount of sesame seeds served

Place pork in roasting pan. Mix all marinade ingredients well in medium bowl, dissolving salt and sugar, and add to pork. Marinate 1 hour in refrigerator, spooning marinade over pork occasionally and turning it a few times. Discard marinade. Preheat oven to 450°F (230°C). Lightly oil inside bottom of another roasting pan, cover bottom and sides with aluminum foil and, placing the pork on the foil, roast in middle of oven until golden brown, 25–35 minutes. Pork is done when juices run clear from a test slice into the middle of the center section.

Tips—Pork tenderloin, about 11 inches long, usually comes two to a package, at a total weight of just over two pounds, in the meat section of the supermarket. This recipe can be used in marinating either one or two pieces. We always roast both pieces as these freeze well. Or you may wish to use the second piece for mock thit rung, the recipe for which appears in the chapter "Byways and Backwaters of Vietnam". An oiled and foiled roasting pan will make cleanup easier and any trickles of marinade which may be baked onto the pan are more easily removed if you pour boiling water over them. Note the label when buying pork loin for this recipe, to be sure to avoid those preseasoned with "flavoring solutions." If you've had sesame seeds long they can become rancid because of their oil content. A quick sniff tells you if that's happened and they should be discarded.

For Red Hot Lovers Only

Hong Kong's flavorful and memorable Cantonese cuisine is about the most mild and unembellished of all the regional styles of the China Seas and China as well. While garlic, chili, spices, gravies, and stewing may dominate elsewhere, the Cantonese favor a more subtle, though never bland, approach, often based on chicken broth. While the multi-faceted nature of Hong Kong's international and regional restaurant industry affords ample opportunity to find a fiery Sichuan or Thai favorite, a Cantonese would be inclined to side-step that in favor of something less assertive.

I enjoy about every dish set before me; a holdover from the days when kids ate what was on their plate and learned that if you sat and looked at something long enough it would begin to look fairly non-toxic. In later years, exposure to spicy scorchy specialties in Pakistan, Mexico, Sichuan and Thailand eased my transition into a confirmed chiliholic, that culinary nirvana where you just simply like it *hot*. In Sichuan restaurants the condition is sometimes referred to as having "a mouth of steel."

Texans generally claim a high level of immunity to the more incendiary varieties of hot chili, reputedly munching raw wild ones like candy. Some Texans actually carry along their own stash of dry chili flakes when traveling far from home, which brings us to a little scenario which took place near the coast south of Bangkok. Lunching at the country home of a Thai friend, with a Texas couple who had arrived in Thailand that very day, as the first dish was set before us the wife pulled a little silver shaker from her purse.

"I never travel without my chili pepper flakes," she said. "We're from *Texas* and we like our food *hot* and *spicy.*"

It was one of those grand times when you know what's going to happen next and you just can't wait.

Our host politely warned her, "Thai food is quite spicy and this first dish is particularly hot."

"Not like in Texas," she beamed, vigorously showering her chili flakes over the plate. She took a bite.

You can bet she never did that again. Not in Thailand anyway.

Even confirmed chiliholics learn to show some respect at the upper levels of the chili food chain. For example, there is the little dried pequin which, if you saw one on your kitchen counter, it might cause you to suspect there is a mouse on the premises. The pequin is officially rated at around half the lava level of the fiery habanero, arguably the world's hottest.

You're more likely to encounter the pequin in villages and back street eateries around the China Seas than in the better-known tourist resorts. Restaurant operators tend to shun it, perhaps fearing it might traumatize their unsuspecting clientele. The pequin is often confused with its cousin, the tepin, which is round, while the pequin is somewhat oblong.

Daughter Lisa found pequins growing atop seaside cliffs in Saipan when she was living there. The pequin is descended from those macho little firecrackers from Oaxaca and Yucatan in Mexico which, it is likely, made their way west across the Pacific and the China Seas in the days of the old Manila-Acapulco galleon trade.

One of my favorite chili memories took place on a sunny afternoon at a little open-air beach-side restaurant following a hike from home along the shore of Hong Kong's Repulse Bay. I'd ordered a steamer of shrimp and a saucer of soy sauce, reminding the waiter to add a half dozen sliced fiery little green Thai chilies to the soy dip. These are the common short thin red or green chilies, known also as birdseye, and are shaped rather like the little finger of a lady at afternoon tea. As the shrimp arrived in a shroud of steam I plopped one into my mouth with a nibble of chili. At that instant I became aware of a half dozen Cantonese of college age at the next table who were watching in gleeful anticipation of the anguished antics which follow when unsuspecting foreigners come up against these demon chilies for the first time.

The standard scene involves shrieks and wheezes as the victim slumps slack-jawed into the chair, sinuses flowing like the Yangtze in spring, with eyebrows aflutter. But none of that happened. I chewed contentedly, locked in their gaze, as their smiles, one by one, slowly faded.

Swallowing with a smile, I nodded and said softly, *"Ding gua gua."*

In collective wide-eyed awe they muttered, *"Ding . . . gua gua?"* Popping another shrimp/chili molar melter, I repeated with resolve, *"Ding gua gua. Wonderful."*

If you're inclined to take up this chili challenge, remember to show respect. Marinate the chilies a couple minutes or so in the soy dip dish. Dip the peeled shrimp into the soy, pop the shrimp into your mouth with just a *nibble* of chili. Once you're in this league you've earned the right to say *ding gua gua* with a flourish. To underline it you can add *la bu pa,* which means "hot not fear."

A dish which goes well with this not-soon-forgotten dip is. . . .

GARLIC SHRIMP
serves 2
Ingredients
½ pound raw shrimp, unpeeled

6 medium garlic cloves, peeled, finely minced or passed through a garlic press

2 to 3 lettuce or cabbage leaves, for the steamer bottom as a bed for the shrimp

Cut an incision with the tip of your sharpest knife, not quite halfway through the shrimp, along the length of the shrimp's back, almost to the tail. If the shrimp has been deveined, just deepen the incision slightly. Stuff the incision with garlic. Place shrimp on a bed of flattened lettuce or cabbage leaves in the steamer, cover and set over boiling water in a bamboo steamer about 5 minutes, depending on size of the shrimp, until just rosy pink. Place the steamer on a plate and bring to the table steaming hot. Remove steamer lid at the table.

Tips—Thawed, individually quick frozen shrimp from the supermarket, either peeled or unpeeled, may be used for this and it is well to keep these handy in your freezer for use in Asian soups, stir-fries or whatever. Any number of dips go well with garlic shrimp; a Chinese or Thai chili sauce or a soy dip with chopped or minced chilies, perhaps with a touch of sesame oil and/or spring onion. Unpeeled shrimp afford a more informal, outdoorsy China Seas ambience and shrimp in the shell holds the garlic better. When serving unpeeled shrimp, have bowls on the table for discarding shells. With finger foods such as shellfish, in addition to damp, chilled, tightly rolled washcloths, provide a large bowl of warm black tea and a few thin slices of lemon to serve as a finger bowl. The tea and lemon slices, rubbed over the fingertips, help take away the fishy smell. Shrimp cooked in the shell is even more flavorful than peeled shrimp.

The Secret's in the Sauce

There's an old story, fondly told in China involving hungry royalty, nostalgia and hushpuppies. Well, maybe not exactly hushpuppies from the American South. Perhaps something more like corn fritters. The Chinese name, *xiao wo tou,* conveys the idea of looking like little beehives.

The story centers around the Empress Dowager Cixi, a woman who fares badly in Chinese history. Her notable indulgences, including the diversion of defense funds to build her summer palace and callous corruptness and incompetence helped hasten the downfall of the Qing, China's last dynasty. An event which probably pleased just about every Chinese outside the imperial household and its system but it did nothing to enhance the old girl's place in history.

The story involved her being obliged to take refuge in a peasant home during her escape from the foreign armies which swarmed into Beijing from the coast in response to the Boxer Rebellion that she had supported.

At the home, tired and hungry, the monarch ate some simple little steamed cakes made from cornmeal and went on her way. Two years later, able to return to Beijing, she recalled that provincial snack and instructed the royal kitchen to prepare it for her.

Unfamiliar with such a plebeian dish, and having some trouble shaping and steaming cornmeal, legend holds that the imperial chefs had to go out to see how villagers did it. Putting their talents to work, and probably burning some good luck joss at the temple, the cooks embellished their creation a bit and added ground chestnut, an imperial favorite since early days.

At dinner, a hush of anticipation descended as the dish was set before the empress. After a few tentative bites and a roll of her eyes, she clucked, "This is exactly as I remember it." It really wasn't quite what she had before but as the Chinese say, "Hunger is the best sauce."

Steaming and shaping cornmeal is more an artform than a food science, perhaps best left to grandmothers in northeastern Hebei province. But with help from friends, while the recipe proved easier than I'd expected, after some 70 years of sloshing around in kitchens, I found it the most notably fluid and tenacious "dough" I've encountered.

Having traveled widely in every province of China over the years, I have seen the little cakes only at the Old Imperial Dining Room in Beijing's Forbidden City, where the waitress momentarily relaxes her decorum and with what passes as somewhat of a flourish in the sedate surroundings, she relates that Cixi story.

If you're curious about trying a little something which one of China's last royalty found to her liking, this is about how it was made. . . .

XIAO WO TOU
Serves 3 to 4
Ingredients
1 cup yellow fine-ground cornmeal
2 tablespoons all-purpose flour
2 teaspoons sugar
½ teaspoon salt
½ teaspoon baking powder
10 +/- tablespoons tepid milk

Add cornmeal to medium bowl. Sift together into the bowl the remaining 4 dry ingredients and with a large wooden spoon mix well. Add milk, a tablespoon at a time, blending it in with fingers, and continue slowly until the mixture can be shaped into a dome in the bottom of the bowl. Cover with plastic wrap and let it rest 10 minutes. Amount of milk depends on the moisture content of the meal and flour, so if the mixture is overly-dry or a bit too moist, slowly add scant additional milk or meal to correct to the point at which you can shape it into a ball which holds its shape. This will be a very sticky mixture. Cover the ball again and let it rest another 10 minutes. Knead it a bit to make it more elastic and divide in half. Divide each side into about 5 equal pieces. If you have the moisture right you will be able to gently form it into a small ball. Knead each piece a moment and holding it in the palm of your hand, form it gently into a conical "beehive" shape, while inserting the tip of your other index finger gently into the bottom to make a shallow indent.

As each piece is finished, place it hole-side down on a single layer of white cotton material, cut to fit, on the bottom of a Chinese bamboo steamer. Over a large pot of boiling water, steam the pieces, covered with the steamer's bamboo cover, for 20 minutes. Serve at room temperature on a plate as an appetizer.

Tip—Cornmeal is ground fine, medium or coarse. Fine is recommended, just a bit smaller grind than household salt.

The Atrocious Secret Ingredient

A single day's production in Wanchai's E Sing bakery catapulted owner Cheong Ah Lum from obscurity into Victorian Hong Kong history. Problem was, it led to his arrest and put him out of business.

As the Hong Kong correspondent for the *The Illustrated London News* reported on January 30, 1857, "this atrocious affair" involved Cheong's innovative addition of arsenic to his bread recipe. No lives were lost but 200 to 300 English consumers were reported to have fallen violently ill. It was said Cheong was acting on orders of Chinese officials following an incident three months earlier involving China's boarding of a small British-owned vessel and arresting its Chinese crew. The action catalyzed a mix of events which turned up the heat on what was to become the Second Opium War.

Fleeing to Macau, Cheong was arrested with nine accomplices and was returned to Hong Kong to stand trial. One newspaper account has him and three associates condemned to death and shot. However, another report has them acquitted for insufficient evidence with Cheong being banished for five years. As is typical of history you may simply choose the version you prefer.

The incident perhaps inspired Mrs. Beeton to suggest a few years later in her *Every Day Cookery and Housekeeping Book,* "it is a good plan to change one's baker from time to time, and so secure a change in the quality of the bread."

This brings us to that point of our narrative which introduces a recipe. Though it isn't likely you'd be interested in Cheong's version, Hong Kong bakers have long been noted for the variety and quality of their sweet specialty items. So, the question is, with all the Western and Chinese choices available, what might have been a breakfast and tea treat for the Old Colonials? History is a bit hazy on this point so in order to come up with a recipe and with apologies to Sir Arthur Conan Doyle, let's turn to Victorian London's Baker Street.

"Victoria buns."

"I say, Holmes, how can you possibly arrive at that?"

"Bear in mind if you will, Watson, our propitious acquisition of Hong Kong, as a British Crown Colony, occurred early in the reign of Queen Victoria and the paramount settlement on Hong Kong Island is, in fact, named in honor of our good queen. Victoria Harbour lies to the north, Victoria Peak to the south and Victoria Park to the east, leading us to but one conclusion . . . Victoria buns. Elementary."

Victoria buns were popular in those days and are typical of what you would be served today, along with dainty sweets, scones and tea sandwiches at that memorable and time-honored Hong Kong social indulgence, Afternoon Tea in the gilded lobby of the regal old Peninsula Hotel. . . .

VICTORIA BUNS

makes 8 buns

Ingredients

1 cup all-purpose flour

¼ cup granulated sugar

1 teaspoon baking powder

¼ teaspoon salt

4 tablespoons butter, softened

⅓ cup regular raisins

⅓ cup golden raisins

1 egg, at room temperature, well beaten

In a medium mixing bowl, sift together flour, sugar, baking powder and salt. Gently cut in softened butter with a wooden spoon and/or dough blender, until flour looks like fine dry bread crumbs. Fold in raisins. Add egg and stir gently until dough clings together. Turn out onto a lightly floured board and knead gently 20 strokes. Shape into a ball, dusting with more flour if it is overly sticky. Flatten dough into a circle about ¾ of an inch high. Cut circle in half and cut each half into 4 equal size wedges, for a total of 8 pieces. Place them, about 2 inches apart, on an ungreased cookie sheet. Bake immediately in the middle of a 325°F (165°C) preheated oven 12–15 minutes until bottoms begin to take on a golden brown and a toothpick, stuck into a bun, comes out without any trace of unbaked dough. Serve hot with butter and jam at breakfast or tea.

Tips—To moisten and plump raisins, the evening before baking, run cold water over them, drain well, place them on a plate with just enough water to touch (not cover) them and cover with plastic wrap and set aside until morning. Rinse and drain raisins again in the morning before using them. Even very dry raisins may be reconstituted this way. Dry raisins draw moisture from a batter or dough, producing an overly dry product. Baking powder, once opened, loses strength after 6 months. To test for freshness, stir a teaspoonful into a half cup of hot water. Fresh baking powder produces an active bubbling. To hasten softening of butter, cut it into small cubes.

The Hong Kong Noodle King

Strangely out of place—but still common in the Central district in the 1970s—Hong Kong's stately old Victorian buildings presented a curious backdrop for the growing bustle of international business swirling about them. Imagine a rock concert in an Elizabethan theater. It was something like that. Decibels and all.

Hurrying along one morning with an old friend from Shanghai in the shadow of these soon-to-be-replaced reminders of a romantic past, we pivoted off Des Voeux Road onto Pedder Street and ran into an animated gentleman with a captivating grin who my friend introduced as Harry Wong, adding, "The Noodle King of Hong Kong."

Harry's business card revealed that the title related to his being Director of Winner Food Company, one of Asia's leading producers of food. An innovative merchandiser, Harry opened Hong Kong's first instant noodle factory in 1969. A few years later he introduced MSG-free noodles there, a product widely exported internationally.

With my work in US wheat market development, from that chance meeting, Harry and I were soon spearheading a number of wheat-based-noodle marketing projects. Later, it was Harry to whom I turned for technical and marketing counsel when food industry officials in Beijing requested help in the modernization of China's noodle industry in general, and the introduction of instant noodles in particular. Chen Ine Chiun, an old friend from my earlier days in Taiwan and an associate of Harry, was called in to oversee production and quality. That was a stroke of luck as there are so many different types of noodles produced in China that it would have been most difficult in those days to find anyone who was considered an authority in the field. Chen, however, was recognized as one of the world's leading experts, to the degree he was known as "Noodle" Chen, and no one in China knew more about instant noodle production. Nicknames are widely used among Chinese friends and associates as code names such as "Gold Tooth" or "Sharp Dresser" to make it clear which Chen, Wong or Li you are talking about.

"Noodle" Chen and Harry were so successful in our instant noodle ramen marketing and technical program, a dozen years after the opening of our pilot plant in Shanghai, nearly 800 instant noodle plants had been established throughout China. Even with that phenomenal growth, officials estimated that production at that time was roughly 500 plants short of China's demand for the new product.

Today, instant noodles are one of the most popular foods in China.

Made from wheat flour, the rolled sheets of dough are cut, steamed, fried and dried in the shape of small noodle cakes. The product evolved from the first Chinese noodles introduced into Japan which the Chinese called *la mien,* meaning "stretched noodles" but actually something of a generic term for Chinese noodles. With the lack of differentiation between "l" and "r" sounds in Japanese, this became *ramen.* Today's revolutionary instant noodle ramen was developed in 1958 by the Taiwan-born owner of Nissin Foods who later became a Japanese citizen, Momofuku Ando.

Ramen has become an international food industry phenomenon due to its unbeatable combination of convenience, quality, flavor, economy, variety, shelf life and availability. To prepare it all you need is a pot, water and heat. Or, it can be nibbled right out of the package. It is well-known to people in a hurry, and in America, particularly to college students and to young singles.

The simple instructions on the package leave nothing further to say here about its preparation other than to suggest that with just a touch of panache—

the addition of something like a few shrimp or bits of chicken or pork, perhaps a few peas for color and a garnish of chopped spring onions and/or fresh coriander on top—it can be easily transformed from a quick snack into a real Chinese soup or noodle dish.

For starters, here is a basic dish, pork noodles, which during my teen years was my personal favorite at the little Chinese-American chop suey restaurants of that era.

And almost exactly what you'd find today in Hong Kong, on junks and sampans and in restaurants, homes and at street stalls. . . .

PORK NOODLES
serves 2
Ingredients
2 slices of ½-inch Cantonese roast pork (see page 47), cut into ¼-inch strips
2 packages pork, chicken or Oriental flavor ramen noodles
Sauce
2 flavoring packets from ramen packages, or just 1 packet and 1 tablespoon soy sauce, to taste
Garnish
1 spring onion, rinsed, with roots and top few inches of green tops trimmed off and discarded, lightly chopped

Open noodle packages, setting aside the flavoring packets. Use a pot large enough to lay the noodles side by side flat. Before adding noodles, add enough water to just cover them. Add flavoring and/or soy sauce (see Tip section) when water boils, add and stir noodles. For noodle soup for 2, add 2 more cups of water but if you want noodles only, boil just enough water to slightly cover the uncooked noodles when laying flat. Boil about 3 minutes, stirring noodles gently. Remove noodles into serving bowls. If doing noodle soup, divide soup between the two bowls. Scatter sliced pork strips over top of noodles and garnish with spring onions.

Tips—Make the pork beforehand. Or you can pick it up in an Asian store or in supermarkets with an Asian food section. Or buy a takeout order at a Chinese restaurant. If you prefer not to use the flavoring packets (for less sodium or MSG) you can flavor the dish with soy sauce and, if you wish, a bit of sesame oil, to taste. Or try using chicken stock rather than water. If you do not have a pot large enough for two noodle nests to lay flat side by side, that can be resolved by gently stirring the noodles in a manner which equalizes their exposure to the boiling water.

Byways and Backwaters of Vietnam

Despite our best efforts to encourage Son Mitchell to develop an early interest in the joy of cooking, initially the only thing he ever made in the kitchen was a bee-line for the back door. His interest in things culinary extended only as far as the refrigerator and his idea of food preparation was spreading mayonnaise on a slice of bread. But that likely would occur only on special days, like maybe the Moon Landing.

But by the second grade, living and traveling in South Asia, Mitch got hooked on foods which a less-traveled Western youngster might never encounter in his or her entire life. And if they did, chances are they'd have serious reservations about it, wrinkle their nose, or try to hide it in their milk. Mitch, however, evolved over the years into a first-rate practitioner of Asian cooking, to the degree that he's now at the wok so often it's a wonder he hasn't developed stir-fry elbow.

Visits to Mitch's Honolulu home over the years afforded the opportunity to savor new dishes, to the accompaniment of exotic food stories picked up in his years working in the byways and backwaters of Vietnam.

There's his story involving an American associate who, having ordered cucumber salad in a village eatery, was surprised when the waitress brought him a plate of pickles. Reminding the girl he'd ordered cucumbers, she replied, "Those *used to be* cucumbers."

Another time one of his group, whose command of Vietnamese was notably inadequate, ordered eel under the impression it was a beef dish. The waitress suggested, "You really don't want that." He insisted he did and that's what he got. But rather than tidy slices of yummy finger-size eel, this sea monster—boiled and coiled on the plate—was roughly the size of the American's arm. He looked aghast at the creature's soulful expression as the waitress tilted her head, shrugged and went about her business with a slight smile. It follows the old adage: if your restaurant server suggests you change your order, do it.

Turtle is a popular delicacy, usually served in tasty bits and pieces in a clay pot with vegetables and a rich gravy. Mitch tells of a time he saw it served without being cut up at all. Rather, it was brought to the table stripped naked, on a plate; a whole cooked turtle without its shell. A really quite remarkable and unappetizing sight.

When it comes to the preparation of less exotic but traditional Vietnamese food, I defer to Mitch's counsel. My business days in Saigon in the 1960s were, by design, brief and limited. In those days it was never a question of where the best food could be found but rather which restaurant the Viet Cong was unlikely to blow up that evening. And we never ate at an hour the restaurant was crowded. An unattended briefcase, anywhere, was bothersome, and a clear sign to position yourself behind a sturdy pillar or leave the room altogether.

Politics and pyrotechnics aside, the food in Vietnam proved to be a definite plus. Blessed with dishes long influenced by the French and Chinese, the country's best known and most popular dish is *pho,* a hearty one-pot blend of beef and noodles. Or you might say it is a soup. Or a salad. Actually, it's a little of all three. On a menu it may be listed simply as "Hanoi beef soup."

Pho is pronounced as if saying "fun" without the "n." This is mentioned simply as a point of information. The Vietnamese don't expect foreigners to get it right.

Pho is eaten throughout the country at breakfast, the Vietnamese equivalent of American ham and eggs. In Vietnam Mitch has had it as many as thirty days in a row. And he still likes it. It's that kind of dish.

As is typical of national dishes you find a number of variations on the basic theme. And, as Vietnamese cuisine has become popular in the United States with refugees opening restaurants in Little Saigons throughout the country, Americans have responded with simplified versions of the dish. Fortunately the variations turn out pretty well.

The first *pho* recipe I came across called for a five-hour simmering of four pounds of beef rib bones with the cooked meat then shredded off the bones with a fork. Then it started getting to be work. Something had to give.

A few minor adjustments in counsel with Mitch made the recipe easier and equally pleasing to the palate. . . .

PHO
serves 4

Ingredients

2 pounds of medium oxtail bones, rinsed

3-inch piece of fresh ginger, peeled, lightly smashed or heavily scored with a knife, quartered

1 cinnamon stick

3 star anise or 24 star points

3 whole cloves

½ round white or yellow onion, peeled, lightly chopped

1 medium carrot, peeled, quartered

4 spring onions, rinsed, with roots and top few inches of green tops trimmed off and discarded, quartered

1 teaspoon whole black peppercorns

¾ pound beef flank steak, rinsed

2 ounces crinkly, translucent Chinese bean thread vermicelli noodles (estimate amount from weight shown on package)

3 tablespoons Asian fish sauce, or to taste

2¼ teaspoons salt, or to taste

I teaspoon sugar, or to taste

¼ round white or yellow onion, peeled, sliced paper thin

Garnish

I pound bean sprouts, rinsed

3 spring onions, rinsed, with roots and top few inches of green tops trimmed off and discarded, lightly chopped

6 tips of fresh Asian basil or regular basil and/or watercress or mint, 2 to 3 inches long, rinsed

3 fresh red Thai chilies or 2 medium Serrano chilies rinsed, thinly sliced

8 sprigs fresh coriander leaves, rinsed, lightly chopped

I fresh lime, cut into 4 wedges

Accompaniment

4 tablespoons Chinese chili sauce or Chinese chili garlic sauce

Half-fill a large pot with water, bring to a medium boil and add oxtail bones. When water returns to a boil, boil for 3 minutes. Pour off water and discard, retaining bones. Rinse pot with hot water and wipe it clean with a paper towel. Rinse bones and return them to the pot. Add 2 quarts of water to the pot and add ginger, cinnamon, star anise, cloves, chopped onion, carrot, spring onions, and peppercorns. Bring to a boil, reduce heat to a very low simmer and cook, covered, 2 hours, uncovered I hour, stirring occasionally. Remove from heat and set aside.

While the bones are simmering, wrap beef flank steak tightly (flat) in plastic wrap and place in freezer. After 30 minutes, remove the chilled beef, unwrap the plastic, and with your sharpest knife slice across the grain diagonally as thin as possible. Set aside.

When the pot has cooled enough to handle comfortably, strain soup through a large sieve, discarding bones, vegetables and spices. Retain liquid, strain into pot, skim excess fat from the surface and set aside.

Soften noodles by placing them in a small mixing bowl covered with warm water 20 minutes, stirring 3 or 4 times, until pliable and soft to the bite. Drain and cut noodles into 3 to 4 inch lengths and set aside.

Place bean sprouts in a colander, bring 2 quarts of water to a boil and pour the water evenly over the sprouts to cook them. Allow sprouts to drain in the colander 10 minutes, stirring lightly with your fingers 2 or 3 times to cook more evenly as they cool.

Attractively arrange the rest of the garnish on a large serving plate, add the bean sprouts to the plate and set aside. Briefly return soup pot, covered, to medium-high heat, adding fish sauce, salt and sugar to taste. Increase heat to high. Divide the noodles into individual, large, warmed soup bowls. When the soup comes to a boil, immediately add the sliced round onion and steak, stir once and when the meat just starts to change color, in a few seconds, divide it among the bowls with a large slotted spoon or small sieve. Ladle out and divide the soup into the bowls. Serve piping hot with the garnish and chili sauce alongside in small dishes.

Tips—The Asian ingredients called for will be found in Asian food stores. Oxtail bones may be retained, with the meat being used for another dish, if you wish. Garnish is added to the soup at the table, according to individual preference, with diners giving the lime a light squeeze over the surface of their soup. Garnish is best served at room temperature, as chilled garnish from the fridge will cool the soup. Older bean sprouts may have tiny brown tips. If fresher sprouts are not available you may snip off the discolored tips. Asian basil, found fresh in Asian stores, imparts a spicy China Seas hint of anise.

Thai chili is the common thin green or red variety, also known as Asian chili and sometimes as birdseye. It is shaped like a lady's curved little finger at tea. *Pho* may be eaten with chopsticks, using a spoon for the broth.

*   *   *   *

In the back country years ago Vietnamese friends took Mitch to a village restaurant for *thit rung,* literally "forest meat." Featured were wild pig, barking deer and porcupine, the latter proving the most tasty. The grilled meat was served with a variety of sauces and Mitch's favorite, new to him, was a spicy-hot mixture called *muoi ot,* which translates simply as "chili pepper salt."

Back home in Honolulu Mitch set to work in the kitchen and was able to recreate this hot sauce which he recommends as a dip for a snack of thin slices of hot-off-the-grill meats, particularly pork or beef. Or whatever sounds good to you.

This is a wonderful, yet somewhat rowdy, in-your-face garlic dip which is best eaten by everyone in the group as, otherwise, those who do not eat it will become aware of a disturbing deterioration in air quality. . . .

MUOI OT
serves 2 to 4
Ingredients
1 ½ tablespoons garlic, peeled and finely minced or crushed in a garlic
press
1 tablespoon fresh chili, finely minced
3 tablespoons lime juice
¼ teaspoon ground black pepper
¼ teaspoon salt

Mix well and serve in small individual dishes for dipping.

Tip—Try adding a few drops of Asian fish sauce to this, to taste.

*   *   *   *

Getting wild game onto the table can be a challenge these days unless you're a hunter, know one, or have access to some big-city exotic meat supplier. Fortunately, our daughter Heather's husband, Greg, enjoys mucking through frigid duck marshes at dawn, trudging through ankle-deep snow in elk country and other outdoor primordial pursuits, depending on the season. Heather sees Donald Duck or Bambi in every duck or deer so a fair amount of Greg's success comes our way, with elk and venison finding its way onto the grill and into the *muoi ot* dip.

If you don't have a hunter in the family and find yourself in the mood to try a Vietnamese-style back country snack, you can replicate a hint of wild game with this recipe. . . .

MOCK THIT RUNG
serves 4 to 6 per tenderloin

Ingredients

1 or 2 lean pork tenderloins, rinsed and patted dry with paper towels

Marinade

1/8 teaspoon salt

1 medium garlic clove, peeled, finely chopped or passed through a garlic press

½ spring onion, rinsed, with roots and top few inches of green tops
trimmed and discarded, finely chopped
2 tablespoons Shao Xing wine or good dry sherry
1 teaspoon regular soy sauce
1 teaspoon Worcestershire sauce
⅛ teaspoon ground white pepper

Place pork in roasting pan. Mix all marinade ingredients well in medium
bowl and pour over pork. Marinate 1 hour in refrigerator, spooning
marinade over pork occasionally and turning it a few times. Discard
marinade. Preheat oven to 450°F (230°C). Lightly oil inside bottom of
another roasting pan, cover bottom with aluminum foil and, placing the
pork on the foil, roast in middle of oven until golden brown, 25–35
minutes. Pork is done when juices run clear from a test slice into the
middle of the center section.

Tips—Pork tenderloin, about 11 inches long, usually comes two to a package
at a total weight of about two pounds. This recipe will marinate either one or
two pieces. We roast both pieces as we freeze cooked pork leftovers for up two
months. An oiled and foiled roasting pan makes cleanup easier and any trickles
of marinade which may be baked onto the pan are more easily removed if you
pour boiling water over them. Avoid buying tenderloin labeled "preseasoned
with flavoring solutions."

Cheung Chau's Chummy Cheeky Cockatoo

Hong Kong's tiny island of Cheung Chau had the good fortune of remaining largely unsullied by tourists in the years it was one of our favorite China Seas hideaways. One of those charming out-of-the-way places that time seemed to have somehow forgotten, it maintained its aura of unfettered tranquility into the early 1980s.

One of Cheung Chau's many charms was the fact there were no cars on the island, its winding cobblestone lanes being too narrow to accommodate them. The island's sleek and shiny "fire engine" was slightly larger than a kiddy car.

Now one of Hong Kong's more popular side trips, in those days there were few foreign visitors, even day-trippers. With a population somewhere around 15,000, less than a dozen Westerners lived on the 1½ square mile island and for the most part their crash pads were too small, sparse or Spartan to accommodate more than an occasional overnight friend or two. There were a couple of little old hotels tucked away here and there in the jumble of little lanes but none (even by some stretch of the imagination) presumed to cater to your typical international tourist.

For most Western visitors, creatures of air-conditioned comfort, there wasn't much attraction in enduring an hour's inconvenience on the lurching old Cheung Chau ferry just to see a slice of exotic Old China. In those days—with the mainland of China closed to the foreign devils—there was still plenty of colorful and quaint old stuff to see just outside your hotel in downtown Hong Kong. Lovely little Cheung Chau was simply too primitive and distant for many. The introduction of a speedier, air-conditioned ferry in the 1980s changed that, hurtling our little island hideaway headlong into what we've come to accept as today's real world.

In the early days, with frequent reminders from our old friend Walter Hirsch that his comfy two-bedroom Cheung Chau retreat was underused and always available for an overnight or whatever—when we might find ourselves so inclined—the Lovely Charlene and I made it a point to be so inclined as often as possible.

Except for the resident Chinese, we had Cheung Chau pretty much to ourselves, with the evening ferry transporting back to Hong Kong the last of the day's few visiting *gweilos.*

Cultural footnote—"*Gweilo*" is the Cantonese name for Westerners. Originally a derisive term, it translates as "ghost person," a reference to the foreign devil's pasty face. But the inscrutable Westerners, somewhat to the chagrin of the Cantonese, took to the name and it's long been in common English usage.

While virtually unknown to the outside world in our early days there, Cheung Chau had six claims to fame. Well, seven if you count Percy. First, the place was one of the most colorful of Hong Kong's 230-plus little islands. It had a real pirates' cave and there were Bronze Age rock carvings on the beach below Walter's place. And there were charming old temples, one dating from the late 1700s which is the repository of a famous Sung Dynasty sword. A TV antenna, perched precariously on the old tile roof, signaled that Cheung Chau was on the threshold of change. Another gem in the island's crown was an annual Bun Festival in the spring, one of the most colorful of all South China's religious holidays. A highlight was a parade in which youngsters seemingly defied gravity by balancing on the tip of a sword, a fan or a vase, an illusion created by concealing cunningly-crafted metal frames under the children's clothing. Another memorable attraction of the nearly week-long holiday involved three bamboo towers, some 60-feet high, completely covered with around 20,000 steamed buns. At midnight on the final day, at the single stroke of a gong, the young men of Cheung Chau dashed across the square and clawed their way to the top of the towers, plucking buns as they went. Said to bring good luck, the buns at the top of the teetering towers were considered the most fortuitous.

That brings us to Percy, the chummy, cheeky cockatoo who was considered one of the charms of Cheung Chau by all who knew him. And on Cheung Chau there were few who didn't know the precocious parrot. He was the pet of Colin Stuart. But it was clear—particularly to Colin—that Percy either saw it the other way around or simply considered himself Colin's roommate. A British expatriate (or exile depending on which friend was relating the story) Colin was Cheung Chau's most ubiquitous *gweilo*. The most likely to arrive early and to stay late—so he didn't put a damper on the party—Colin was as solid as a Smithfield ham. Clearly one to side-step in a rugby scrum. He was one of that era's great cast of colorful Hong Kong players who likely would have inspired Somerset Maugham to sit down and get to his writing.

In outline form, we learned—by bits and pieces over the years—Colin was born in London during the Battle of Britain and in his first week out of the hospital his parents carried him up from the bomb shelter three nights in a row only to find that German bombers had destroyed the place to which they had moved. Things could only get better.

After the war, Colin's father, a Royal Air Force senior pilot and doctor was assigned to an island in the Seto Inland Sea near Hiroshima where Colin grew up, fluent in Japanese. Finishing his studies in England, he enlisted in the elite Queen's Life Guards cavalry, later serving in Germany with the First Royal Tank Regiment, after which he joined Scotland Yard. Security work brought him to Hong Kong where he achieved that rarest of accomplishments for a Westerner—fluency in Cantonese.

Percy seemed to think he was in security work also. Hanging in his spacious white cage in the garden, on hearing your approach up the hill, he would whistle and screech "Percy! Percy!" and he'd keep that up until you shouted, "Hello, Percy." Satisfied with the password, he would return to the serious business of sentry duty.

On Colin's walks into town his alfresco feathered friend routinely tagged along behind, hedge-hopping in free flight from branch to bush.

One Sunday passing the garden, I noticed Percy's cage was empty with the door open. Colin, sitting casually in the shade of a banana tree as he browsed a copy of the *South China Morning Post,* nodded toward the south end of the island.

"He's over there."

"How will you get him back?" I asked, catching sight of a tiny white dot high in a distant tree.

"He'll be back. He always comes back."

A neighborhood party regular, Percy screeched and whistled happily along with our rowdy rugby songs and if you'd stand in front of his cage and jiggle up and down with jerky little knee bends, he would do the same, waggling his bright yellow topknot. Not a tango, but Percy had rhythm. And he was voracious where snacks were concerned.

Noting one evening that the personable parrot was dropping most of his pasta I asked Colin if perhaps Percy didn't care for spaghetti. "Loves it," Colin said. "That's just a trick of his to save it for a snack later."

Actually, Percy seemed to like just about everything the rest of us were eating. One of his favorites was Walter's barbecued chicken. And he particularly seemed to enjoy drumsticks heavily basted with a special sauce which Walter had created one day quite by chance with what he had on hand in the pantry when a crowd showed up unexpectedly, which was not at all unusual.

While Percy carried it off with considerable *savoir-faire,* it always seemed a bit odd to see him, balanced confidently on one foot, nibbling casually on a barbecued drumstick which he held up firmly with his, well . . . drumstick.

If he'd had a more extensive vocabulary, he'd most likely have said, "Hey, it's only a *chicken.*"

If you'd like to sample Walter's serendipitous sauce, just as he made it for the Cheung Chau Rooftop Gang and Percy, this is all there is to it. . . .

WALTER'S BARBECUE SAUCE
serves 4

Ingredients

½ cup Grey Poupon Dijon mustard

1 tablespoon celery leaves, rinsed and minced

1 spring onion, rinsed, with roots and top few inches of green tops trimmed off and discarded, minced

1¼ teaspoons black pepper, freshly ground

1½ teaspoons white vinegar

Blend ingredients together well in a bowl and baste on chicken and pork while cooking for a crisp crust.

*   *   *   *

Personable Percy also had a penchant for Guamanian barbecue, that is, the Lovely Charlene's version of the recipe which she acquired during her years on Guam. A combination of chicken and pork with a zingy and aromatic basting sauce of ginger and ketchup, it was one of our lazy Sunday favorites.

Had you dropped by around midday during our decades in Manila, Taipei or Hong Kong, this is perhaps what you would have been invited to sit down and enjoy with us.

Our youngsters, now grown and scattered halfway around the world between the China Seas and New York, continue to provide occasional cultural updates on Guamanian barbecue. Son Mitchell, in a dispatch from his home in Honolulu, noted that our family recipe was milder than the many popular variations in Guam, where the sauce is the foundation of the island's spicy cooking and is called *finadene*. In Guam, most versions you'll see sizzling and smoking on barbecues along the white sand beaches call for three or four hot green chili peppers. And a bottle of beer. Not for the marinade. For the cook.

Lisa has spent much of her life on tropical islands—Guam, Saipan, Majuro in the Marshalls, Luzon in the Philippines, Bali, and St. Lucia and Vieques in the Caribbean, where the word barbecue is said to have evolved from the Indian word, *barbacoa*. Having sifted more warm sand between her toes than anyone else in the family, if a procedural question arises at the grill, Lisa dons her beach barbecue mantle of arbitration.

Lisa notes that while in America you might find the country's favorite beverage—ketchup—on the table, in Guam they'll have *finadene* sauce to liven up rice, soup, eggs, meat and fish. They even put it on Spam which perhaps has something to do with the fact Guamanians consume more Spam than anyone else in the world, just over 20 tins per person per year. Hawaii is the highest in the United States with more than five tins per year. Spam's popularity in those places is a legacy of the Pacific War when the tinned pork meat from America was a luxury for islanders. Lisa's never seen ketchup in any of the versions in Guam and theorizes our recipe evolved out of backyard barbecues on US Navy and Air Force bases there.

The variations on this dish are tempting and virtually endless, but we stick with our mild family recipe which always sets the neighbors to ogling and salivating when the tantalizing wisps of barbecue smoke drift their way. . . .

GUAMANIAN BARBECUE

serves 4

Ingredients

4 boneless lean pork country ribs, rinsed and patted dry with a paper towel

4 skinless chicken drumsticks, rinsed and patted dry

4 skinless chicken thighs, rinsed and patted dry

Marinade

1 medium round white or yellow onion, peeled and thinly sliced

1 blend of equal parts regular soy sauce and white vinegar, about 2 cups of each, sufficient (depending on pan size) to almost cover the meat marinating in a roasting pan

Basting sauce

1½ cups of ketchup

2½-inch piece of fresh ginger, peeled and grated

Place ribs in a large pot with enough water to cover and bring to a boil, reduce heat and simmer 20 minutes. Meanwhile combine onion, soy sauce and vinegar in a large roasting pan. When ribs are done drain and discard water. Allow ribs to cool slightly and add them and the chicken to the onion, soy sauce and vinegar marinade and place in the refrigerator, turning the pieces occasionally while marinating 3 to 4 hours. Meanwhile in a bowl, mix together well the ketchup and grated ginger. When the meat is ready, discard marinade, place meat on a platter or cookie sheet and, with a pastry brush, coat meat with the ketchup and ginger sauce. Place the meat on the barbecue grill over moderately high heat, basting and turning it frequently 20 to 30 minutes until done. Serve hot.

Tips—This may be served with rice as they would do in Guam. For the ginger, use a ginger grater, available in Asian stores and specialty kitchen shops. Made of metal or porcelain it has a flat surface with tiny sharp upraised points which the ginger is drawn across to grate it. Ginger is stringy so remove with a toothpick and discard the stringy little nests which gather during grating. Figuring about three pieces of chicken or pork per person, this recipe can be expanded to serve larger groups by simple adjustments to the amount of marinade and basting sauce. While we have never had any leftover, we have it on good authority that Guamanian barbecue is equally enjoyable hot or cold, eaten with the hands or a knife and fork. But as with watermelon and apple pie it stands to reason it is better eaten out of the hand.

A Man for All Seasonings

Master-Doer-of-Daring-Deeds James Bond was drawn to Hong Kong a number of times over the years and in one death-defying episode he is lured by the forces of evil to—of all places—Cheung Chau, our peaceful little island hideaway west of Hong Kong. In *No Deals, Mr Bond* by John Gardner, Bond sets out to settle the score with General Konstantin Nikolaevich Chernov of the KGB. With Chernov holed up at his fortress villa (just up the beach from our friend Walter Hirsch's place), the outnumbered Bond outwits and outdoes the bad guys and saves his hostage friends. And the world as well, for the time being anyway. A good read.

One of the fun things about writing fiction must have a lot to do with the control one wields over characters, circumstances and unlikely coincidence. Particularly the latter. In what passes as real life, of course, within minutes of Bond's flare going off overhead (KA-Whoom!) instead of being quite alone, he would have been overrun by thousands of tousle-haired, pajama-clad islanders, jostling indignantly and jabbering in a raucous chorus, demanding to know what on earth he thought he was doing. Bond always slips out of tight places but it's difficult to imagine how he might have handled this bunch, a turn of events which surely would have left him both stirred and shaken.

About the most excitement we had come to expect in our many years of holidaying on Cheung Chau was sitting back on Walter's flat rooftop watching the great crimson flame tree create shade.

Food, fun and friends set the tone at Walter's. While you might have the minor inconvenience of a typhoon or a power outage from time to time, or a report of something slithering through the jungled garden, the one thing you could count on at Walter's was eating well.

For snacks there were copious quantities of steamy swollen sausage and crusty hearty breads liberally spread with an imported Muenster which smelled rather like a wet Airedale which had rolled in something it should have buried. It was the best cheese I ever tasted.

Lunch time on weekends usually found a casual ensemble of friends gathered alfresco on Walter's rooftop. The little single-story house was weathered concrete, solid as a bunker, with the flat roof accessed by a narrow stairway from the little dining room.

With our host presiding over the barbecue grill we dawdled and joked over chilled refreshments beneath the outstretched limbs of the gnarled old flame tree. The menu was usually chicken, pork, or shrimp, all acquired fresh from the open-air waterfront market at the bottom of the hill.

At other times the Lovely Charlene prepared bouillabaisse, thick with the catch of the morning from the local fishing fleet. She accompanied this with a never-ending supply of hard rolls, which in bite-size chunks assumed the function of a soup spoon. With a crisp amber crust, the rolls were purchased hot, fresh and fragrant at a tiny nearby bakery and were as flavorful as any you'd find in Europe or San Francisco. With only an archaic brick oven which lacked any modern steam-injection capability, we speculated how the crunchy crust could have been set so well. The suggestion that it could perhaps be accomplished by the baker spraying a mouthful of water over the rolls as they went into the hot oven was summarily rejected by all hands.

Using the recipe for what had become known to the Cheung Chau Rooftop Gang as Charlene's bouillabaisse, Walter—on occasions when we were away—prepared this savory seafood spectacular himself and before long he was referring to it as *Walter's* bouillabaisse, setting the stage for the Great Cheung Chau Bouillabaisse Debate.

This, of course, goes right to the heart of the ancient alchemy of this seafood stew which varies from country to country, kitchen to kitchen, the seasonings on hand, or whatever the catch of the day may be. Arguably most popular of all fishermen's stews, the curious thing about bouillabaisse is that despite any individual or day-to-day variations, it somehow manages to retain its delightful character.

My wife finally was moved to chide Walter for usurping *her* recipe. Insisting *his* was *different,* Walter noted firmly, "I use more pepper."

A Libra, with the stick-to-it-ive-ness of an overly upset octopus, my five-foot-three wife was not about to let Walter get away with that and continued to hassle the poor guy until he produced his recipe in written form. Neatly typed.

Comparing the recipes, we found that Walter had doubled some quantities and halved others. Well, that *was* different. Also, Walter's called for eight fish heads. The Lovely Charlene, with a roll of those big blue eyes, was the first to agree *that* was *really* different. It seemed a rather clear checkmate for Walter but rather than concede, my wife chose simply to accept the culinary equivalent of a shaky armed neutrality. From then on she and Walter simply took turns at the bubbling cook pot on bouillabaisse days so there was no question as to whose bouillabaisse was coming up. It always came out about the same, to the delight of the Rooftop Gang.

As for Walter, on a first-name basis with the headwaiters and executive chefs in Hong Kong's finest restaurants and a collector of early Chinese blue-white porcelain, it was perhaps inevitable that with his "more pepper" and seven other bouillabaisse spices and herbs, including a whole jar of saffron and another jar of dry parsley, the Cheung Chau Rooftop Gang (including my wife) happily concluded that Walter is indeed a man for all seasonings.

Anyway, the bouillabaisse wasn't actually the Lovely Charlene's as it had come to her by way of a friend. . . .

"CHARLENE'S" BOUILLABAISSE

serves 6

Ingredients

⅓ cup olive oil for cooking

2 cups round white or yellow onion, peeled, thinly sliced

3 medium garlic cloves, peeled, minced

4 carrots, pared, chopped

1 pound of tomatoes, peeled, coarsely chopped or 14.5-ounce can of diced, peeled tomatoes

2 bottles (8 ounces each) clam juice

⅓ cup dry white wine

2¼ cups tomato juice

½ teaspoon saffron, crumbled

1 teaspoon dry thyme, crumbled

½ teaspoon fresh orange peel, grated

1 teaspoon salt

½ teaspoon black pepper, freshly ground

½ teaspoon fennel seeds, crushed

1 bay leaf, well crumbled

2 tablespoons fresh parsley, rinsed and minced

4 pounds fresh firm-fleshed white fish, cut in serving size pieces, bones intact or fillets cut into bite-size pieces, rinsed

2 pounds cooked crab, in the shell, cleaned, rinsed, cut into serving-size pieces

1 pound fresh shrimp, shelled or unshelled

2 dozen clams, in the shell, scrubbed

1 dozen mussels, in the shell, scrubbed and beards removed

Garnish

4 sprigs fresh parsley, rinsed, chopped

Accompaniment

2 loaves French bread, sliced for dipping

Heat oil in large kettle. Add onion, garlic and carrots. Sauté 5 minutes stirring occasionally. Add tomatoes, clam juice, wine, tomato juice, saffron, thyme, orange peel, salt, pepper, fennel, bay leaf and parsley. Low boil 10 minutes stirring occasionally. Layer fish on top of mixture. Cover and boil 10 minutes. Quickly layer crab, shrimp, clams and mussels over fish. Cover, boil 10 minutes more until shells open. Stir seafood into soup. Remove from heat. Garnish either in pot or in serving bowls and serve at once with French bread.

Tips—If the fishmonger hasn't already cleaned out the crab's gunky insides, have it cleaned at the time of purchase. (I learned how to do this in San Francisco 70 years ago but it's a chore best side-stepped if you can.) Remove and lightly crack the claws and legs, cutting the body section into six pieces. For easy peeling boil fresh tomatoes one minute and then plunge them into ice water a few minutes. Then peel. In grating orange peel, do not grate past the colored part. When scrubbing clams and mussels under cold running water discard any with cracked shells or which will not close tightly. Or do not open by themselves when cooked. Place bowls on the table for shells and bones and provide each diner with a chilled damp washcloth. A large communal bowl of warm black tea with a few thin slices of lemon may also be provided to rinse and freshen fingers after eating. These are hearty servings so if no members of the Cheung Chau Rooftop Gang show up at your place, this recipe could serve perhaps eight or nine people.

A Haunting Memory of Macau

The old Bela Vista, perhaps the most charming hotel in the China Seas, was long one of Macau's more venerable reminders of earlier days when the tiny Portuguese enclave was one of the world's richest ports. It had long been the West's only trade channel with China.

Built as a private residence around the 1870s, later a hotel, painstakingly restored to its former grandeur in the 1990s, and since 1999 the residence of the Portuguese Consul, the Bela Vista is one of Macau's most remarkable, historic and best loved structures. It sits high on a wooded hill above the broad sweep of Sai Van Lake (formerly Praia Grande Bay) and its tree-lined promenade. The hotel—with only four regally-appointed suites and four guest rooms—exudes the air of an opulent aristocratic residence.

On our holidays to Macau, to escape the crunchy bustle of Hong Kong, we often stayed at the Bela Vista. Entering the tidy little two-story lobby always seemed something of an Alice in Wonderland rabbit-hole tumble into an earlier and now lost era.

The intimate dining room with its brass chandelier and slowly revolving ceiling fans headed our long list of "most favorite" places to dine in Macau. After a day of exploring dusty little shops and old open-air markets in the meandering cobblestone lanes we usually ate late, savoring every quiet moment as if we were time-travelers transported to a gossamer golden era of long ago.

It was on just such a night that we experienced our most unforgettable evening at the Bela Vista. The curious chain of events was set in motion when the hotel manager, an old friend, joined us for a chat as he often did as we dallied over after-dinner coffee and a notable old port. Comparing notes on Macau's unique cuisine, the enclave's history, and the history of the old hotel, I ventured a long-held question: "Given the long and colorful history of this place, how is it there is no resident ghost?"

With a quick glance over his shoulder he confided, "Actually, there are two."

The Lovely Charlene was fascinated. "Two ghosts? The hotel has two ghosts?"

"Captain William Clarke, the British steamboat captain who bought the place and turned it into a hotel in 1890."

"And his wife?" I ventured.

"His dog. They turn up on occasion after dark in one of the suites."

"A dog ghost? What on earth do these two do?"

"They just sit on the bed. On the headboard."

"They sit on the headboard?"

"That's the story. They don't bother anybody."

As details of various sightings were confided we became aware of a silence settling over our shadowed solitude, with our quiet conversation the only sound in the room. Staff people had been slipping quietly home as we talked. It was the end of another day in Old Macau.

Dispatching my last sip of port, we exchanged goodnights and left the dining room. We encountered no one in the unlit hallway which opened into the quaint, dark, little lobby; now empty and still except for the sound of our footsteps echoing eerily off the hardwood floor through the dark shadowy hallways.

Reaching the top of the stairway, a greenish glow suddenly burst and flickered around us for an instant as a flash of lightning launched a rolling growl across the city.

As we entered the room I quickly closed the door, locking it firmly, making a determined effort not to dwell on the possibility of our being the only guests in the little hotel that night. Within minutes, snuggled under the down comforter, I was stirred fully awake by the realization that our doorknob was turning slowly. Back and forth. Back and forth, just as doorknobs do in scary movies. Rejecting my first impulse to simply pull the comforter over my head and let my wife deal with it, I rushed to the door and looked into the peephole to see who was there.

There was no one.

In the next instant our lights went out and I could feel icy fingers brushing the back of my neck as lightning flashed, sending eerie shapes lurching wildly through the room. Fumbling for my travel flashlight, I splashed a narrow beam of light across the headboard. Nobody there. So far so good.

The phone rang.

"Sorry, our watchman will switch your lights back on. He checked your room, thought it was unoccupied and turned them off."

We don't believe in ghosts. Never did. Well, maybe just for an instant on that night long ago in Macau.

Looking back, the historic old port city has changed considerably in recent decades. Much of the picturesque old skyline and pastel architecture is lost. And, the Bela Vista was taken over by the Portuguese government to serve as the official residence of their Consul when Macau reverted to Chinese control in December of 1999.

But, knowing where the locals eat and how to find the remaining old byways and shops and fun places, we always look forward to our next visit.

In the meantime I slip into our kitchen, when the mood strikes, to recreate one of our favorite dishes, rekindling memories of those grand days in grand Old Macau. . . .

CALDO VERDE SOUP

serves 6

Ingredients

3 tablespoons vegetable oil for frying

2½ inches of mild chorizo or Portuguese style pork sausage, precooked, in the casing, sliced into ¼ inch pieces

1 medium round white or yellow onion, peeled, coarsely chopped

2 medium size leeks, rinsed, with roots and dark green part and first outer leaf removed and discarded, rinsed and coarsely sliced

1¼ cups of ham, coarsely cubed

2 cups of potatoes, peeled, coarsely chopped

4 cups canned chicken broth

1 bay leaf

2 cloves

⅛ teaspoon black pepper, freshly ground

¼ cup extra virgin olive oil

1¼ cups frozen spinach, shredded into thinnest possible strips

Accompaniment

12 to 18 hot soft dinner rolls

butter

¼ cup extra virgin olive oil

Place oil in heavy saucepan and over medium heat sauté the sausage, onion, leeks and ham 3 to 4 minutes. Add potatoes and chicken broth and bring to a low boil. Immediately add bay leaf, cloves and pepper. Reduce heat, cover pan and simmer until potatoes are done. With a slotted spoon, discard bay leaf and cloves. Remove sausage and ham and set aside. Pour soup in blender and liquefy. Return soup to pan, stir in olive oil, spinach, sausage and ham and simmer gently uncovered about 5 minutes. Give a final stir and serve hot with rolls.

Tip—Serve rolls and butter along with the extra virgin olive oil in a cruet so guests may add a few drops to their soup and rolls.

Small Chow at Henri's

An Old China Hand may do it from time to time but most people—even the locals—are disinclined to suggest which one of Macau's many great old restaurants is the best in town.

The former Portuguese enclave—a Lilliputian peninsula and two small islands forty miles west of Hong Kong—seems blessed with more top eateries per capita than anyplace else in the world. That's quite something considering there are some 500,000 people shoehorned into Macau's eight square miles.

Some of Macau's better eateries are hidden away in the old city, up winding cobblestone alleys or nestled in villages on the outskirts. Just when you think you have it pretty well worked out, someone tells you about yet another outstanding hidden gem which has somehow escaped your attention. The cuisine has memorable overtones of African, Indian, Malayan and European, typically on a base of either Portuguese, Chinese or Macanese.

Then, there is the spinoff, "Portunese," which some consider to be the ultimate. This is said to have evolved in the early days when Portuguese men married local girls and set up little eateries as a sideline. Though the lines between Portunese and Macanese are hazy, it's never been much of an issue among people preoccupied with good eating.

In our frequent visits to Macau we never had a breakfast, lunch, dinner or snack that was anything less than outstanding, whether the restaurant was snuggled in an untidy little lane or tastefully appointed in one of the top hotels.

Henri's, on the tree-lined Avenida da Republica on Macau's old seafront promenade is a place we particularly enjoyed lingering long over lunch or dinner. On occasion we'd have both lunch and dinner there in a single day.

Henri Vong opened the restaurant in 1976. Born Wong Yun Ching just across the border in China he localized his name when he immigrated.

Getting to Henri's can be tricky. The place is known variously as Henri's, Henri's Galley, or The Galley, while old hands are inclined to call it Maxim's. The problem is, Macau's cab drivers and tricycle rickshaw peddlers only on rare occasion recognize the English name of any place you want to go. Pointing it out on a map seems to make matters worse.

The inclination of drivers—as holds true throughout much of Southern China—is to simply take off with you aboard, expecting you to tell them where to turn or stop. It seems reasonable to assume you can get to Maxim's by using the Chinese translation, *Mei Xin.* But that doesn't work either. What does work is the Cantonese *Mei Sam.* If you have the hotel desk clerk write that out for you or ask the doorman for help you will miss a memorable cross-cultural exchange with your driver, along with a fascinating back street tour into areas you would otherwise never see.

As small as Macau is, it's sometimes easier to abandon the cab and walk to your destination.

Meals at Henri's always started with what the waiters called "small chow." This was Henri's spicy shrimp and his thinly sliced Portuguese sausage flamed at the table with *bagaceira* brandy. These appetizers were savored along with hot-from-the-oven Portuguese bread rolls to the accompaniment of an icy bottle of dry white *dao reserva* wine.

One evening as Henri chatted at our table I reminded him that he had given *Gourmet Magazine* his African chicken recipe when they requested it and it seemed only fair that he give me his small chow shrimp recipe for my cookbook.

Henri agreed that for a longtime customer that seemed only fair. . . .

HENRI'S SMALL CHOW SHRIMP

serves 2

Marinade

1 tablespoon Chinese chili garlic sauce

1 small garlic clove, peeled and minced or passed through a garlic press

1 teaspoon smooth regular peanut butter

2 tablespoons dry shredded sweetened coconut

1/8 teaspoon salt

1/4 teaspoon black pepper, freshly ground

Coating

2 eggs well beaten with fork

1 1/2 cups fine dry bread crumbs

Ingredients

1/2 pound uncooked rock shrimp (or similar medium shrimp) shelled

1/2 cup peanut oil for frying

Accompaniment

Chinese chili sauce

Blend together in bowl chili garlic sauce, garlic, peanut butter, coconut, salt and pepper. Pat shrimp with paper towel and add shrimp to marinade and refrigerate 1/2 hour. Mix together eggs and 3 tablespoons of water. Place bread crumbs in medium bowl. Dip shrimp individually into egg and water mixture and dredge in bread crumbs, placing coated shrimp on wax paper. Repeat dipping and dredging one more time until all shrimp have a double coating. Warm wok over medium high heat about 2 minutes until a drop of water falling onto it makes just one sizzling bounce. Add oil and increase heat to high and when oil begins to shimmer and light haze (not smoke) begins to rise, add shrimp and gently stir-fry until golden, about 2 minutes. Place shrimp on paper towel a moment to drain. Serve hot along with individual little soy sauce dishes of chili sauce.

Tips—For better blending of the coating, first mince the shredded coconut with a knife, kitchen shears or a food processor. Shrimp should be small, about the size of a cashew, peeled and deveined. Raw shrimp is best. If using cooked shrimp you must be careful and just heat it rather than overcook which toughens shrimp. If using larger shrimp, cut them into cashew size. We keep frozen shrimp on hand in the freezer as it comes in handy when doing Asian cooking, as an appetizer, a main dish, or to dress up a soup or noodles. You can buy frozen shrimp either raw or cooked, peeled or unpeeled.

*   *   *   *

The methodology of Henri's equally popular flamed sausage appetizer requires no pondering, practice or confidentiality. As with sweeping a floor or chewing gum there's no trick to it.

A model of simplicity in ingredients as well as in preparation, this rendering affords the sausage as pleasant a fate as any sausage maker could hope for. . . .

HENRI'S SMALL CHOW SAUSAGE FLAMBÉ

serves 2

Ingredients

4 inches of mild chorizo or Portuguese style pork sausage, precooked, in the casing, cut into ⅛-inch coins

2 tablespoons brandy or rum, 151 proof (75.5% alcohol) for flaming

Accompaniment
6 hot soft dinner rolls
butter

Pour 151 proof brandy or rum into a small heat-proof pitcher and place pitcher in a bowl of very hot water and set it aside for 10 minutes or more to warm up. Place sausage slices in ungreased frying pan and stir over medium heat until fat particles in the sausage become translucent and sausage turns darker. Transfer at once to a warm enamelware or other heat-proof serving plate or bowl and place on a hot pad or trivet on the table and immediately carefully drizzle the heated brandy or rum over the hot sausage in a thin circular motion. Touch it with a burning match to flambé it.

Tips—Don't use an excessive amount of brandy or rum and if you have more flame than you prefer simply cover the serving plate with a lid to extinguish it. Exercise caution when pouring to prevent the liquid in the pitcher from catching fire. Sausage should flame only about eight seconds. This can be eaten with a fork or chopsticks without the rolls but it makes a zesty little do-it-yourself finger sandwich.

An Adventure Close to Home

This starts halfway around the world from the China Seas in the editorial office of *Cook's Illustrated* magazine in New England, once home of the tall ships of America's early China trade. Stick with us as our course leads straight to Singapore.

Christopher Kimball, publisher and editor of *Cook's Illustrated,* is on firm ground when he suggests cooking is about studying other people. It's a passport into other cultures. And the rewards are great, broadening one's horizons, expanding friendships and international understanding while enhancing appreciation of the First Happiness; the joy of eating well.

After visiting a huge Vietnamese supermarket in California, Kimball enthused, "It was like dying and going to heaven—the ultimate gourmet supermarket . . . a memory difficult to erase."

Kimball is onto something here. Over the years I've noted that Western customers you come across in Asian food stores in America often have something of what you might call a kid-in-the-candy-store look about them.

These shopping sojourns make me feel like a kid on an Easter egg hunt, wondering what seasonal surprise or new item I may come across here, there or around the next turn.

Then there are the people you never see in these stores. People who are interested in getting into Asian cooking but lack the know-how and are reluctant to take those first uncertain steps through the beaded curtain into a real Asian food store; an exotic place of strange labels and curious provisions.

How do you go about finding a good Asian food store outside Asia? You aren't likely to come across many small communities which can support one, so look in major population centers. Rather than relying solely on the phone book, ask an Asian, preferably one who looks like they cook. That most likely would be someone like a matronly grandmother or a housewife, browsing a supermarket aisle. Or look in the phone book and call an Asian consulate. It doesn't matter if you ask a Chinese, Korean, Japanese, Vietnamese or whatever. They will know where the good stuff is and popular shops tend to have an inventory representative of a wide range of foods and condiments from different Asian countries. Put this question to two or three different local Asians and you will have a short list of the best places to find virtually any Asian ingredient a recipe may require; certainly any this cookbook calls for.

Happily, today many Western supermarkets offer a fair selection of standard Asian ingredients and even some fresh produce which was pretty much unavailable until just a few years ago. I recall as a teenager during World War II in San Francisco, making frequent sojourns into neighboring Chinatown, where, for example, the only litchi nuts available were dried and unappealing. It wasn't until decades later when I got to China and had fresh ones that I learned how wonderfully juicy and sweet they are. It was even greater than the difference between a mushy thawed strawberry and a firm succulent freshly-picked one.

To really relish the variety and joys of Asian cooking at home today, if you haven't yet made an initial solo sojourn through the aisles of an Asian food store you should do it soon. It's simple and fun. The shop people are usually quite pleased to see someone new from outside their usual ethnic circle. Take your time so you can browse and ask questions. It's part of the scenario, even for Asian customers.

Despite labels written in a variety of Asian squiggles many products carry English names or can easily be identified through their clear glass or plastic containers. Labels now often carry English translations. When making a selection always take note of the "best before" date, particularly in the little shops where some inventories move slowly.

If you live or travel in the Far East, you can avail of one of the most culturally broadening of all arenas, the open-air market. All you need for your first shot at this is to have a spirit of adventure or a resident friend or associate who'll show you the ropes. Best have your money in small denominations as food stalls tend to have trouble changing large bills. Having the right change is particularly essential in the fish market where currency tends to drip and perhaps smell like an outdated mackerel.

If you want to fly solo on foreign shores have someone teach you the phrases "how much?" and "too much" and how to count. That is essentially about all you need for basic open-air market haggling. Further communication can be reduced to simple finger waggles, frowns, smiles and nods. The Chinese have hand signals for numbers from one to ten. Have someone teach you these, as they come in handy when haggling in Chinese markets, and it gives the appearance that you really know what you're doing.

The hand signal system is particularly helpful in differentiating between the numbers four and ten in Chinese as they sound pretty much the same when spoken by a foreigner.

There is no reason to be nervous if you go it alone. I don't know of anyone who disappeared in one of these places or who was ever bitten by the merchandise. Although there was the Taipei Snake Shop Incident. This involved my boss who was visiting from the home office in America. Somehow I came up with the idea that he might enjoy the novelty of roaming around a live snake shop, an unsettling repository of reptiles, which tends to cause the hair on the back of a Westerner's neck to stand straight up on end and tingle. There are all manner of poisonous snakes of all sizes in wire mesh cages in the narrow aisles, awaiting their fate as snake soup, snake wine, or as a medicinal tonic. Now, if you have ever looked a cobra straight in the eye, close up, it's easy to imagine what heinous thoughts about you are coursing through its evil little sociopathic brain. And we were surrounded, eyeball-to-eyeball, with cages full of them. Stooping for a closer, cautious, creepy look, we failed to notice this monkey in a cage on the floor alongside the snakes. Apparently in a playful mood, the monkey suddenly snaked-out his long thin black arm, grabbing the boss' finger in a lightning-fast blur which we barely caught sight of. Fortunately, the boss and I both somehow warded off a coronary arrest in the second or two it took to realize that what had him was only a monkey. I was inclined to feel it was also fortunate that the boss had agreed earlier that he too thought the snake shop visit might be fun.

It was a memorable example of point of view. I snickered about it the rest of day but the boss never did once. Returning home late, I slipped into bed and snickered a couple times in the dark which awakened the Lovely Charlene who asked what the heck that was all about. I related the story and we both snickered ourselves to sleep.

Roaming Asian markets anywhere, it is easy to get the impression shopkeepers haven't noticed your presence, but they have and they tend to be protective of foreigners in their midst. On one occasion in Hong Kong, I accidentally dropped a HK$100 bill (about US$13) and would have been totally unaware of it if it hadn't been for a little old Cantonese shopkeeper who tugged at my sleeve and pointed it out to me. We then proceeded (to our mutual enjoyment) to have a good finger-waggling haggle over the price of her quail eggs.

Shopping at a vegetable stall in Taipei in one of those big old barn-like neighborhood markets, the owner was engaged in a masterful job of making it appear he had not taken any particular note of my presence, a technique applied when they really want to give a stranger the once-over. Slowly he tilted forward, squinted and laughed. Pointing to the small monogram in Chinese which I'd had embroidered on the pocket of my denim jacket, he asked if I could read it.

"Sure. It means I'm afraid of my wife." That doubled him up.

Saying you are henpecked is an inside joke among Chinese, the inference being that if you say you are the boss at home, it's highly unlikely you are. But if you insist you aren't, then perhaps you are. But most likely not.

Waving to other merchants the stall owner shouted, "Hey come see what's written on his pocket." Everyone was delighted with my repeated assurance that the Lovely Charlene was indeed the boss. And I couldn't help but notice that the prices I was quoted in that market from then on were particularly reasonable.

On your initial shopping sojourn in an Asian market, it helps if you have a shopping list or recipe in hand. And if you're stumped or curious, you'll find the clerks or other customers are equally pleased to offer counsel or to help you find something.

If you enjoy seafood put together a shopping list from the following recipe and try this easy and delightful chili crab, a China Seas favorite which is one of Singapore's most typical and popular dishes. . . .

SINGAPORE CHILI CRAB
serves 2 to 4
Sauce
1 egg, well beaten with a fork

2 tablespoons sugar

¼ teaspoon salt

1 teaspoon regular soy sauce

8 tablespoons ketchup or a blend of 4 tablespoons ketchup and 4 tablespoons Chinese chili garlic sauce

1 tablespoon Mekhong whiskey or light rum

Ingredients
1 cooked Dungeness crab, about 1½ pounds, in the shell, cleaned, rinsed,

cut into serving size pieces, or 16 cooked crab claws, with the shell lightly
cracked

7 tablespoons peanut oil for frying

Seasoning

2-inch piece fresh ginger, peeled, quartered

4 medium garlic cloves, peeled and finely chopped or passed through a
garlic press

3 fresh red Thai chilies, finely chopped

Accompaniment

1 cup hot cooked rice per person

Garnish

2 sprigs fresh coriander leaves, rinsed and lightly chopped

In small bowl, beat egg and set aside. In a medium bowl, mix sugar, salt,
soy sauce, ketchup and Mekhong, stirring until sugar dissolves. Set aside.
Warm wok over medium high heat about 2 minutes until a drop of water
falling onto it makes just one sizzling bounce. Add oil and increase heat to
high and when oil begins to shimmer and light haze (not smoke) begins to
rise, add crab and stir-fry 2 minutes. Remove crab from heat, retaining oil
in wok. Turn down heat and set crab aside on paper towels on a plate.
Return oil to medium high heat, add seasoning and stir-fry until garlic just
begins to change color. Immediately add crab and sauce and stir
continuously, coating each piece of crab, 2 to 3 minutes. Remove from
heat and stir in egg well. Turn crab out onto serving dish and garnish with
coriander.

Tips—Thai chili, also known as Asian chili or birdseye, is the common short
red or green thin chili with a slightly arched shape like a lady's little finger at
afternoon tea. The crab is eaten with the fingers. Set a bowl on the table for

empty shells and provide each diner with a damp chilled washcloth. A communal bowl of warm black tea with a few thin slices of lemon may be provided to rinse and freshen fingers after eating. Diners may spoon extra sauce from the serving bowl over their hot rice. Mekhong whiskey is difficult to find outside Southeast Asia but if you or a friend are going to Thailand, this can be found virtually everywhere there, including airport shops.

The Number One Dish—Appetizers

In Hong Kong honored guests are presented at lunch, dinner or a banquet with appetizers of some consequence. When it comes to breakfast, Hong Kong's *dim sum* breakfast is made up entirely of appetizers. With roaming carts of delicacies from which to choose, it's the World Cup of appetizer experiences.

Even a simple lunch or dinner at home usually begins with a small dish or two of family favorites and, with the exception of open-air food stalls, it would be a rare eatery which did not offer customers at least one complimentary little dish to begin the meal. Often this is a house specialty and quite likely a major attraction for customers, much like the engaging spicy yet sweet pickled cabbage at Hong Kong's popular Red Pepper restaurant in Causeway Bay. Waiters there know to bring me a second dish along with the menu.

Some of the really fancy restaurants feature a kaleidoscope of first course banquet cuisine, centerpieced with a plate-sized butterfly, bird or dragon artistically rendered in a variety of colorful, thinly sliced and sculpted vegetables and meats. The guest of honor is expected to cast the first chopstick to begin the decimation of the little work of art.

For meals at home there are a number of tasty appetizers which require only a few minutes in the kitchen. The following are some family favorites. Quantities may be adjusted upward if you are having guests. These dishes aren't highly structured or tricky so if you prefer something a bit less salty, maybe more tart or sweet or whatever, make adjustments to suit your taste.

Appetizers may be served in small individual dishes or bowls or arranged on a large serving plate, family style. For ease in handling while appetizers chill in the refrigerator, marinate each in a sealable plastic bag rather than in a bowl which takes more space and tends to be tippy when shelves get crowded. Plastic bags may be stacked and turned over from time to time for more even marination. And clean up goes faster with disposable plastic bags.

Remember, for food to be the First Happiness the cook should be happy too, so keep it simple with one or two of the following appetizers. . . .

COLD MARINATED CELERY
Ingredient
2 cups of celery, rinsed, sliced into 1-inch lengths with bottoms and leafy tops removed and discarded or an equal amount of Chinese celery
Marinade
¼ teaspoon salt

1½ teaspoons sugar

1¼ tablespoons regular soy sauce

2 teaspoons sesame oil

Place celery in medium saucepan, cover with cold water and on medium high heat, bring to a low boil. Boil 1 minute. Drain into colander and immediately plunge into ice water to retain texture and color. Drain, pat dry with paper towel and set aside. In sealable plastic bag mix salt, sugar, soy sauce and oil and agitate to dissolve salt and sugar. Add celery, mix well and chill in refrigerator at least 1 hour, swirling and turning occasionally. Just before serving swirl, drain, and serve cold.

SWEET AND SOUR RADISH

Ingredient

3½-inch section from the smaller end of a white Chinese radish, peeled and sliced as thin as possible into coins. Or 3 to 5 large red radishes, sliced thin, unpeeled

Marinade

1 tablespoon sugar

½ tablespoon red wine vinegar

2-inch piece of fresh ginger, peeled, sliced into quarters and lightly mashed

Place radish in sealable plastic bag. Add sugar, vinegar and ginger. Swirl bag to mix well and set aside to marinate at room temperature at least 1 hour. Swirl and turn occasionally. Just before serving, swirl and serve cold.

Tip—This calls for the long white Chinese radish, which the Japanese call *daikon*.

VINEGAR-SOY CUCUMBER

Ingredient

5-inch section of cucumber, cut in half lengthwise and then sliced into ½-inch coins

Marinade

1 tablespoon cider vinegar

1 tablespoon regular soy sauce

In sealable plastic bag, combine vinegar and soy sauce. Add cucumber, swirl to coat evenly and agitate bag a few times over the next 10 minutes and then drain out the marinade. Then refrigerate at least 1 hour, swirling and turning occasionally. Just before serving swirl and serve cold.

Tip—The long firm seedless English (hothouse) cucumber is particularly suited for this dish.

COLD MARINATED ASPARAGUS

Ingredient

1 pound thin fresh asparagus

Marinade

1/8 teaspoon salt

1 teaspoon sugar

1 tablespoon regular soy sauce

1 tablespoon sesame oil

Rinse asparagus and holding both ends, bend each stalk so tender top snaps off about 5 or 6 inches long. Discard tough ends or freeze and save for later use as soup stock. Place asparagus in large saucepan of water at a rolling boil and when water returns to boil, cook for just 1 minute. Drain into colander immediately and plunge into ice water to retain texture and color. Drain well and pat dry with paper towel. Combine salt, sugar, soy sauce and sesame oil in sealable plastic bag and agitate to dissolve salt and sugar. Add asparagus, swirl gently and refrigerate 1 to 2 hours, swirling and turning occasionally. Just before serving swirl, drain, and serve cold.

SPRING ONION FLOWERET
Ingredient
6 spring onions, rinsed, with roots trimmed off and discarded

Cut 3-inch section from the white root end of each onion, discarding the rest. From the white end, slice straight down carefully toward the green end with your sharpest knife making 5 or 6 crosshatch cuts 1 inch deep. Chill in the refrigerator in a bowl of ice water at least ½ hour before serving, with enough water that the flowerets have room to open. The sliced ends will curl into little flowerets. Drain and pat dry gently with paper towel before serving cold as an appetizer or garnish.

Tip—Unused green sections of onion may be chopped and used as garnish for soup or noodles.

Chop Suey du jour

Chop suey endures the dubious distinction of being the best known yet least understood of all dishes you'll find in a Chinese restaurant in the US.

It would appear that just about everyone has heard about chop suey. But as is often the case with things Chinese, what the foreigner believes he or she understands is at odds with reality.

It goes something like this. Fairly early on, chop suey seems to find its way into the vocabulary of Western youngsters with the subtext that it's something of a staple among the Chinese. It comes as a surprise later to learn that we were wrong; that there's no such thing in China and it's actually a sort-of-Chinese creation of the Overseas Chinese restaurant industry.

No matter what anyone tells you to the contrary, even your very own mother, chop suey is indeed a Chinese dish. Trust me. Read on.

The fanciful legends about chop suey are legion. An American friend tells of being taught in high school that chop suey was invented by Chinese cooks as a mock Irish stew for laborers laying track for the transcontinental railway. Another story credits its creation to a Chinese housekeeper in early San Francisco. As the story goes, when his employer returned home late with friends and asked for Chinese food the housekeeper whipped up a dish which delighted everyone. Asked what it was, the housekeeper said it was "*chop suey,* leftovers." That isn't what it means but the legend persists.

If you happen to have a number of Chinese cookbooks it's quite unlikely you'll find a recipe for chop suey in any of them. We have nearly 60 Asian cookbooks and the only one which includes chop suey is the first one we acquired on moving to Taipei in 1972. This is the refreshingly unpretentious first volume of *Pei Mei's Chinese Cook Book,* written by Taiwan's internationally acclaimed food authority, teacher and one of the early TV chefs. She footnotes that chop suey is an old Guangdong dish, *li kung cha sui.*

Typically, otherwise-authoritative books simply state it "really isn't" a Chinese dish. Cookbook authors perhaps refrain from including a recipe because readers might infer the author can't be much of an authority on the cuisine if he or she thinks chop suey is Chinese.

In China, to be sure you have the correct answer to your question you need to put your question to three or more people. Asking individuals tends to work better than putting the question to a group. That's how Old China Hands go about getting answers, often finding it necessary to then divide the responses by two or maybe two and a quarter in order to work out the answer.

Much of the confusion stems from asking the wrong question or putting it to the wrong person. If you ask if they have "chop suey" in China the answer will be, "No." Properly put, the question is, "In China do you have a popular dish of chopped and mixed stuff something like our chop suey?" They do, lots of them.

I long ago lost track of the number of times I've heard visitors in Hong Kong ask the host at a 14-course dinner, "Do you eat like this at home every night?" The answer, to the amazement of the visitor, is always, "Yes." What the host means is, at home they have egg flower soup, beef with oyster sauce and stuff like that. But not all at once.

In China, chop suey has a number of popular local hash-house counterparts which have long provided students and laborers with an inexpensive fast food. Yes, centuries ago the Chinese invented that marketing marvel we know today as fast food. The chop suey concept may apply to any chopped and mixed dish. Fried noodles and fried rice are members of the clan.

A few decades ago, Mongolian barbecue restaurants began appearing around the China Seas and in recent years they found their way to the United

States and have enjoyed a growing popularity. The way this works is, from a cafeteria-style display case, customers fill their bowl with their choice of raw meat, vegetables, fruit or pasta and condiments and the restaurant grills it.

Lunching at a Mongolian barbecue restaurant recently, the Chinese manager, an old friend from Taiwan, joined us for a chat and I ventured, "What your customers are putting together here is actually chop suey."

"Exactly."

"And when the major ingredient they choose is pasta, they are creating a personalized chow mein." He agreed.

True Mongolian barbecue evolved from early northern nomads and hunters, cooking their food by campfires on hot stones and the ingredients were basically lamb and onions with perhaps some tomatoes, a few leaves of spinach, garlic, chili, ginger with splashes of rice wine, and soy sauce with perhaps a coriander garnish. Stuff you find on the Silk Road. That's pretty much how we do it. But if you want to add some pineapple, fish or other oddities, that's fine. The idea is to enjoy it and not fret about form.

Although chop suey is widely viewed and generally served in the West as a rice dish, it may be served over noodles. Or, as is often the case when it appears in Chinese homes, chop suey may be prepared simply as a side dish, along with (or over) rice or noodles, without adding meat or seafood. Chow mein is simpler in concept, translating simply as "fried noodles" so it came as somewhat of a surprise to those with some grasp of Chinese cuisine and the language when, in the 1980s, the genius of American marketing came up with a canned chow mein "without noodles." This proved popular enough to be followed by the introduction of a canned chow mein *"with* noodles."

A friend's parents operate a restaurant in Honolulu where the father confided to me, "Chop suey is the one dish no customer can complain about because nobody knows what it is supposed to be."

When Chinese order chop suey in an overseas restaurant they may specify that it be "Chinese style." That is, as the cooks would make for themselves. I have heard Chinese inquire of the waiter, "What kind of chop?" Or, they may specify "big" chop which calls for a wider array of ingredients than the restaurant's regular rendition.

In the mid-1980s it came as a surprise to note that chop suey began appearing on menus in a few international restaurants in Hong Kong, probably in response to tourists' requests. For the adventuresome gourmet, if you look around Hong Kong you can even find chop suey *soup* on a menu.

Chop suey's naturalization process in the gold fields and railroad construction camps of the early American West began as Chinese laborers—not chefs—tried to imitate their native style of home cooking. With the limited Asian ingredients at hand, this required a high level of inventiveness. Some years ago in the mountains of Idaho an abandoned old rice terrace was discovered, a leftover from the days Chinese miners combed the back country for riches. Anyone who has attempted Chinese cooking without such standard ingredients as ginger, sesame oil or star anise can appreciate the problems these pioneers faced.

As these early Chinese sought other sources of economic survival, in their cloistered little Chinatowns, there arose Chinese laundries and chop suey joints which were to become an integral part of Americana. Today, for our cardboard-container-carrying-Chinese-chow-crowd, the phrase "Chinese takeaway" has become almost redundant, reflecting the popularity which has been attained by this blend of East and West.

However, as jovial Wang Shu Wie, director of the Shanghai Food Bureau, suggested, "Whether it's Chinese food in America or American food in China, the challenge for both is in getting it just right."

But, don't be dissuaded, here's an authentic Chinese chop suey, which comes from our family friend, Pansy Lam of Hong Kong, who we had to ask to write it down for us, as traditional dishes such as this are made almost by instinct, without referring to a recipe. . . .

CHOP SUEY

serves 2 to 4

Marinade

2 tablespoons regular soy sauce

¼ teaspoon ground white pepper

1 teaspoon sugar

1 teaspoon cornstarch

Ingredients

⅓ cup uncooked boneless lean pork loin, fat trimmed off, sliced into ¼-inch thick, bite-size pieces

1 tablespoon peanut oil for frying

3 medium garlic cloves, peeled and finely chopped

⅓ cup small shrimp, cooked and shelled

1½ tablespoons peanut oil for frying remaining ingredients

1½ tablespoons oyster sauce

4 spring onions, rinsed, with roots and top few inches of green tops trimmed off and discarded, coarsely chopped

3 dried black Chinese or shiitake mushrooms, soaked 20 minutes in warm water, quartered with stems trimmed off and discarded

1 small carrot, pared, sliced into 2-inch matchstick-size slivers

½-inch piece of fresh ginger, peeled, cut into 5 coins

1 cup cabbage, coarsely chopped

¼ cup green bell pepper, seeds removed, sliced into matchstick-size slivers

Accompaniment

1 cup hot cooked rice per person

Garnish

2 sprigs fresh coriander leaves, rinsed and lightly chopped

1 spring onion, rinsed, with roots and top few inches of green tops trimmed off and discarded, finely chopped

Mix marinade ingredients well together in a medium bowl until sugar dissolves. Stir in uncooked pork and place in refrigerator for at least ½ hour, stirring occasionally. When ready, stir again and strain pork through a sieve, retaining marinade, and set aside. Warm wok over medium high heat about 2 minutes until a drop of water falling onto it makes just one sizzling bounce. Add 1 tablespoon oil to wok and increase heat to high and when oil begins to shimmer and light haze (not smoke) begins to rise add garlic and stir-fry until garlic just begins to change color. Immediately add shrimp and stir-fry about 30 seconds to heat through. Remove shrimp and garlic from wok with slotted spoon or wooden spatula and set aside, retaining oil in wok. Add 1½ more tablespoons of oil to wok. Add marinated pork and stir-fry until cooked through and color changes, about 2 minutes. Remove wok from heat, remove pork, retaining oil in wok, and set pork aside. Reduce heat to medium high. Give marinade a quick stir and add it and oyster sauce to wok. Continue stirring while immediately adding in sequence one at a time—and stir-frying each for 30 seconds before the next ingredient is added—the onion, mushrooms (squeezed to remove excess water), carrot and ginger. Add cabbage and stir-fry for about 1½ minutes until cabbage is somewhat pliable. Immediately add shrimp, garlic, pork and green pepper and stir-fry about 1½ minutes until pepper begins to soften. Immediately place in serving bowl, add garnish, and serve hot along with the hot cooked rice in a separate bowl so guests may help themselves to a serving of rice, topping it off with chop suey.

Tips—The foregoing step-by-step guide is not how a Chinese wife would do it. She would simply start chopping, adding and frying whatever she had picked up at the morning market, going at it just as she had seen her mother do it. That is how it is done. Until you've gained experience with a wok, when dealing with a number of ingredients and current events appear to be gaining the upper hand due to the high heat, pull your wok off the heat for a moment. The same applies if the oil should begin to smoke. If the oil in the wok is cooking down more than you would like add another tablespoon of peanut oil. It's a good idea to arrange your ingredients in proper sequence within easy reach and that is particularly true when dealing with many ingredients, as is the case with this recipe. A Chinese would likely retain the water in which mushrooms have soaked and add it to a soup or perhaps to flavor another dish, discarding the last two or three tablespoons which may contain some sediment.

Fried Rice Deserves More Respect

Chinese fried rice is taken altogether too much for granted. It's likely that the annual per capita consumption of fried rice is greater than any other dish in the world. This very day carloads of it will be consumed in homes and restaurants throughout the Far East and in every Chinese restaurant in the world. Variations of it are virtually national dishes in other countries, such as Indonesia's popular *nasi goreng*.

Rice was the first cultivated crop in human history, dating back perhaps 10,000 years. Archaeologists have found sealed pots of rice in China almost 8,000 years old. Its 40,000 varieties are a dietary staple for about two-thirds of the people in the world and rice provides around 30 percent of the world's calories. It's been worshipped as a god and throughout history has been a main dish on royal tables in several cultures.

Like life, fried rice is pretty much what you make of it. It may contain shrimp, chicken or pork, perhaps pineapple or fish or crab, depending on the price, the preference or religion of the region, the inclination of the cook, or the day's leftovers from lunch. Ingredients will vary from one household, or day, to another and it could be quite a challenge to find two homes using exactly the same recipe, although the end products may look alike.

We came by our fried rice recipe in a rather unusual way, involving the Kowloon-Canton Railway, the venerable old rail line between Guangzhou and Hong Kong. Making my way along to the dining car years ago, a Chinese gentleman waved and said, "I know you."

"Sorry, I can't quite place you," I confessed. "Was it Nanning? Wuhan? Qinghai!"

He grinned. "I'm Billy Tam. I run the Golden Sampan restaurant and I've seen you there." Holy smoke. The Golden Sampan was about a fifteen-minute drive from our place on the Oregon Coast where we spent our summer vacations before retiring there in the early 1990s. The odds on that encounter being roughly a billion to one, it reinforced my conviction that one should never be surprised at anything that happens to you in China.

A Cantonese restaurateur, born in the rice basket of Guangdong province, Billy qualifies as a fried rice expert in my book, so the following summer on our next visit to the Golden Sampan I asked Billy how he prepares this dish when he is back in the motherland. To my surprise, because Americans tend to prefer their ethnic foods as Americanized as possible, Billy prepares his fried rice at home exactly the same as he does for his American customers.

He stresses the importance of making this with cold cooked rice so it is less sticky and blends easier with the other ingredients. Cook the rice in the evening and refrigerate it overnight. Hong Kong cooks and Overseas Chinese restaurants prefer a long-grain rice which is less sticky than short-grain rice. Short grain is popular in Japan and has the advantage that its stickiness makes it easier to deal with when using chopsticks. Basmati and jasmine rice are widely considered the cream of the long grain crop. A word about instant rice: This works fine for a number of dishes, particularly if you're in a hurry. But if you're in that great a rush, send out for a pizza and do Asian food another time.

While there are more opinions than hard and fast rules in the rice cooking rule book, you will find long-grain rice requires less water in cooking than short grain. When a long-grain rice is cooked with too much water, it does get sticky. So when making fried rice with it, if you have a problem, next time try using an eighth less water.

The secret of making perfect rice is to follow the directions on the package. If the result isn't quite what you had in mind, adjust accordingly next time, using just a little more water if it is too chewy or a little less if too mushy. Add a little butter and salt to taste.

For some reason, Chinese fried rice seems to compel fork-wielding foreigners to assault it mercilessly with soy sauce. Mercy. Traditionally, fried rice should be white or virtually so. If you ever see an Asian engaged in slathering food with soy sauce anywhere around Hong Kong and the China Seas you can bet it's a foreign-born tourist.

Billy's recipe calls for a little soy sauce, but if you're inclined to add more, just remember the wisdom of Omar Khayyam on another subject, "Gently brother, gently, pray . . ."

TAM FAMILY FRIED RICE
serves 4 to 6

Ingredients

¼ cup cured ham, diced

⅓ cup Chinese roast pork, diced

½ cup cooked shrimp, peeled and diced

1 egg, well beaten with fork

¼ teaspoon salt

1 teaspoon peanut oil for frying egg

2 tablespoons peanut oil for frying remaining ingredients

1 spring onion, rinsed, with roots and top few inches of green tops trimmed off and discarded, coarsely chopped

4 cups cold cooked rice

2 tablespoons regular soy sauce

½ cup frozen green garden peas

salt to taste

In small bowl mix ham, pork and shrimp. Set aside. Season egg with salt. Warm wok over medium high heat about 2 minutes until a drop of water falling onto it makes just one sizzling bounce. Add 1 teaspoon of oil to wok, increase heat and when oil begins to shimmer and light haze (not smoke) begins to rise add egg and quickly scramble over high heat with wooden spatula breaking up egg into small moist bite size pieces. Set egg aside. Quickly wipe out wok well with a paper towel. Add 2 tablespoons of oil to the empty wok and return wok to heat. Stir-fry onion 30 seconds. Add ham, pork and shrimp and stir with wooden spatula to uniformly heat, about 2 minutes. Add egg with spatula until well mixed, about 2 minutes. Fluff rice with a wet hand to break up clumps, adding about 1 cup at a time to the wok blending it in constantly until rice is uniformly mixed and heated. Add soy sauce and stir to uniformly mix. Gently fold in frozen green peas. Add salt to taste. Place in serving bowl and serve hot.

Tips—Cantonese roast pork recipe appears on page 47, or pick up a package of Chinese barbecue pork at an Asian store. Leftover pork may be used as a cold appetizer. The pork may be prepared a day or two ahead and refrigerated. Or, simply pick up some barbecued pork from a Chinese restaurant or the supermarket on your way home.

This Food isn't for Sissies

Perhaps there's something in their drinking water or maybe it's their cold wet highland nights. Whatever it is, when it comes to the warrior class, the Scots of the Black Watch and the Nepalese Gurkhas are as tough as they come. As the final days of Empire played out in Hong Kong, these two battle-hardened bastions of the British Army were the last to serve the Crown.

The Black Watch regiment dates from 1725 and served with distinction in the Crimean War, Waterloo, the Boer War and both World Wars. They fought alongside American colonial troops to dislodge the French during the French and Indian War.

Scotland's favorite foods will probably forever remain something of a mystery to non-Scots. I've never had the opportunity to visit the country and have never come across a Scottish restaurant but my wife is a Ferguson and on occasion wears a Ferguson tartan scarf secured with a Ferguson brooch. But she never prepares Scottish dishes.

Having asked around for some time, about all I've come up with so far is that, given a choice, Scots will indulge in treacle, mince, stovies, potted hock, boiled bacon and haggis. While the latter is one of the most ancient of all prepared foods it fell from favor when clay pots overtook animal stomachs as the cooking utensil of choice.

Scots also are partial to Cullen skink, a renowned fish chowder from the village of that name. James Smith, who was manager of the Hong Kong Hilton for more than a decade and an authority on just about everything to do with Scotland, volunteered his recipe. . . .

CULLEN SKINK
serves 4

Ingredients

2 teaspoons butter for pot

½ cup medium white or yellow onion, peeled and diced

½ cup celery, diced

1 cup cream

3 cups canned chicken broth

⅛ teaspoon black ground pepper

⅛ teaspoon lemon juice

⅛ teaspoon thyme

1 cup potatoes, peeled and cubed

4 ounces of skinless smoked haddock, flaked, removing any bones

salt to taste

In large pot sauté onions and celery over light heat in butter, stirring until onions begin to become translucent. Add cream, chicken broth, pepper, lemon juice and thyme. Add potatoes. Simmer and stir occasionally until potatoes soften and the soup begins to thicken, about 10 minutes. Add smoked haddock and simmer 10 minutes. Salt to taste. Serve hot.

Tips—If smoked haddock can't be found at your supermarket, visit a seafood specialty shop and request finnan haddie or finnan haddock, as it is more commonly known, named for the Scottish fishing village of Findon.

*   *   *   *

In the course of researching Scottish foods someone confided that Scots also relish cock-a-leekie, a particularly tasty chicken soup with leeks. An early version of this recipe appeared in 1865 in the first printing of the classic *Mrs. Beeton's Every Day Cookery and Housekeeping Book.* It's difficult to imagine any British housewife of that day setting out for Hong Kong—halfway around the world—without a copy of England's indispensable culinary bible.

This is how Mrs. Beeton wrote the recipe more than a century ago. . . .

COCK-A-LEEKIE

A capon or large fowl (sometimes an old cock, from which the recipe takes its name, is used), which should be trussed as for boiling, 2 or 3 bunches of fine leeks, 5 quarts of stock, pepper and salt to taste.

Mode—Well-wash the leeks (and, if old, scald them in boiling water for a few minutes), taking off the roots and part of the heads, and cut them into lengths of about an inch. Put the fowl into the stock, with, at first, one half of the leeks, and allow it to simmer gently. In half an hour add the remaining leeks and then it may simmer for 3 or 4 hours longer. It should be carefully skimmed, and can be seasoned to taste. In serving, take out the fowl and carve it neatly, placing the pieces in a tureen, and pouring over them the soup, which should be very thick of leeks (a *puree* of leeks, the French would call it). *Time*—4 hours. *Sufficient* for 10 persons. *Seasonable* in winter.

Note—Without the fowl, the above, which would then be merely called leek soup, is very good, and also economical. Cock-a-leekie was largely consumed at the Burns Centenary Festival at the Crystal Palace, Sydenham, in 1859.

Following Mrs. Beeton's basic approach, for six servings, try this. . . .

Ingredients
3 cups canned chicken broth
1 Rock Cornish game hen
2 bay leaves
1½ teaspoons dried thyme
4 slices thick cut bacon, coarsely chopped with excess fat trimmed and discarded
5 medium size leeks, rinsed with roots and dark green part and first outer leaf removed and discarded, coarsely sliced
½ cup barley
2 tablespoons butter
salt and pepper to taste
Garnish
2 tablespoons fresh parsley, coarsely chopped

Add chicken broth to large pot. Add Cornish hen, bay leaf, thyme, bacon and half the leeks and give a quick stir and bring to a boil. Reduce heat and simmer uncovered 1 hour turning hen a few times. In the meantime add barley to 1½ cups of water, boil 10 minutes, drain and set aside. Turn off heat, remove hen and cool until it can be skinned and thoroughly deboned by hand into bite-size pieces. Set aside. Return heat to simmer, add remaining uncooked leeks and the drained barley to pot and simmer

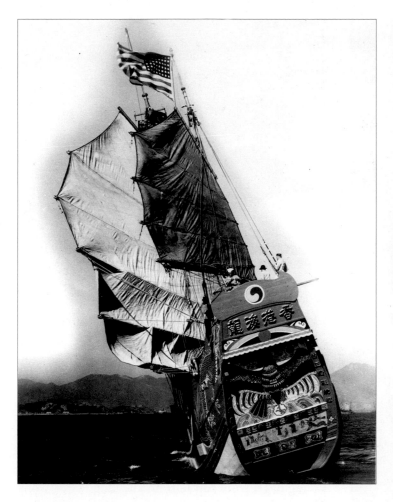

Clockwise from above: the *Sea Dragon*, shortly before it was lost in a Pacific storm on its way to the San Francisco World's Fair; an 1883 engraving of tea in a Hong Kong garden, on the site of where my office would be located a century later; the E Sing Bakery in Wan Chai where a plan was launched to hopefully rid Hong Kong of the foreign devils.

Clockwise from left: a China coast fishmonger with the day's catch; with Mitchell, Heidi and Lisa in hand, we explore a downtown lane – now long gone – in Old Hong Kong on our Asian arrival in 1964 at Chinese New Year; converted junks afforded a respite from the crowded city, along with the opportunity to impose my cigar-box ukelele on an anchored captive audience.

Facing page, from top left: noodle king Harry Wong (left) and "Noodle" Chen in Shanghai, launching China's first instant noodle plant in 1982; Cheung Chau's no-nonsense kitchen, with everything just inches away, affording a convenience like that of a U-boat galley; Percy, Cheung Chau's charismatic cockatoo, demonstrates for Daughter Lesli the aplomb with which he dispatches a chicken drumstick; New Year shoppers in Old Taipei in 1974 serve to illustrate how easy it was to keep track of the Lovely Charlene in a crowd.

Favorite Asian flavor enhancers which are called for in this book's recipes. They'll be found in well-stocked supermarket ethnic sections and Asian food stores.

PICKLED ONIONS – recipe on page 156

SOLE MEUNIÈRE – page 226

HARD-BOILED QUAIL EGGS – page 246

GARLIC SHRIMP – page 51

CHINESE PORK SPARERIBS – page 172

VICTORIA BUNS – page 58

15 minutes. Return deboned hen to pot and add butter. Add 2½ cups water to thin soup. Restore heat and simmer covered 5 minutes. Add salt and pepper to taste. Remove bay leaves and serve at once with fresh parsley garnish.

* * * *

With the Gurkhas we have another elite among elites. No other group of soldiers serving a foreign flag has approached the popularity of these scrappy warriors. They've fought in every major and most minor British wars since they were first enlisted out of their native Nepalese hills on India's northern frontier in 1815. Calling for reinforcements in a sticky situation, British officers traditionally request "British or Gurkha." British officers who have served with the Gurkhas are inclined to boast a bit about it.

Gurkha food is similar to that of north India and depending on the tribe or region reflects Hindu, Buddhist and animist restrictions. Serving overseas, Gurkha troops are excused from diet restrictions except for beef which may not be eaten in any form. Returning home, Gurkhas undergo a purification ceremony before again taking up a tribal diet.

The following dishes are gratefully received household recipes handed down from families of the Queen's Gurkha Engineers Regiment in Hong Kong. . . .

CHICKEN CURRY
serves 4
Ingredients
2 chicken thighs
3 chicken breasts

¼ cup vegetable oil for frying

1 large white or yellow onion, sliced

3 medium tomatoes, chopped

½ teaspoon chili powder

½ teaspoon turmeric

1 teaspoon salt

1 tablespoon fresh ginger, peeled and grated

½ tablespoon fresh garlic, minced or passed through a garlic press

2 tablespoons fresh coriander leaves, rinsed and chopped

½ teaspoon ground cardamom

½ teaspoon ground cloves

½ teaspoon ground cumin

Accompaniment

4 cups hot cooked rice

tomato chutney

Skin and cut chicken from bone into bite-size pieces. In large pan heat oil and fry chicken on medium high heat, about 5 minutes, stirring occasionally. Add remaining ingredients. Stir well and cook another 5 minutes, stirring occasionally. Add ½ cup warm water and cover pan. Simmer 20 minutes on low heat, stirring occasionally. Remove pan from heat, stir and let curry stand about 2 minutes. Transfer to a serving bowl and serve with boiled white rice and tomato chutney (from the following recipe) in separate serving bowls.

Tips—Look for a ginger grater at a kitchen specialty shop or Asian store. Ginger is stringy and in grating, pesky little nests will accumulate. Discard these with the help of a toothpick. Note there is no curry powder in this curry recipe. This is not uncommon in Indian cooking. The word "curry" comes from the Tamil word *karhi* which means sauce, and it has come to refer to a variety of spicy, gravied, Indian dishes, whether the recipe contains curry powder or not.

Chutney is the time-honored accompaniment to curry. Those unaccustomed to Indian food might have a little trouble at first, trying to figure out just what chutney is all about, as it appears in so many different forms. It can be mild or spicy hot and made from vegetables or fruit. It can be salty or sweet with textures ranging from smooth to chunky. Sweeter chutneys serve as bread spreads or as an accompaniment to cheese.

TOMATO CHUTNEY

serves 4

Ingredients

¼ cup vegetable oil for frying

¼ teaspoon fenugreek

¼ cup fresh ginger, peeled and finely chopped

3 medium tomatoes, chopped

¼ cup garlic, peeled and chopped

½ teaspoon turmeric

1 teaspoon ground cumin

⅛ teaspoon chili powder

⅛ teaspoon salt

2 whole cloves

Garnish

1 small fresh green chili, finely chopped

Place oil in heavy saucepan on medium heat and fry fenugreek about 1 minute, stirring occasionally until it turns red. Add ginger and stir into the fenugreek 1 to 2 minutes until ginger darkens slightly. Add tomatoes and stir in over medium high heat about 8 minutes. Reduce heat and add garlic, turmeric, cumin, chili powder and salt and simmer about 5 minutes, stirring occasionally, until garlic takes on a translucence. Add cloves, stir in and simmer 1 or 2 minutes longer. Serve hot. Or this may be made a few days ahead of time and when cooled, store it in a covered glass bowl in the refrigerator. Add chopped green chili to taste and reheat before serving.

Tip—This chutney may be more oily than you prefer in which case simply pour off any excess.

*	*	*	*

Over the course of a few days in December 1941 the forces of Imperial Japan proved that Fortress Hong Kong was indefensible. The fact that the gun emplacements all faced the wrong way, out to sea—as they did in Singapore—is only part of the story. Some of these abandoned fortifications are still in evidence today on the south slope of Hong Kong Island, a few having been converted into private gazebos.

I asked a friend in the British military, "What is the single most overwhelming factor in Hong Kong's indefensibility?"

"The one which matters most," the major twitched, "is the fact there's no way we can get enough troops in here to properly defend this little place."

Aside from the demographic realities, the British military played a major role in the development, security and livability of Hong Kong from the very beginning a century and a half ago. As members of that vast international cast of roving players who shaped this little place into one of the most successful economic entities of all time, the Scots and Gurkhas strode their hour on the Hong Kong stage and then, on cue, duty done, saluted smartly and, to the skirl of bagpipes, marched away forever.

*   *   *   *

From the Khyber to the coast, the Indian subcontinent offers a wonderful and wide selection of native and regional breads which are not only flavorful but are typically used as functional utensils, displacing the Western fork or spoon at meals. The easiest and quickest of these is the very flat, fried, whole wheat chapati, a staple among the subcontinent's warrior classes since the beginning of civilization.

The chapati recipe serves two, but calling only for whole wheat flour, salt and water, it is easily doubled or tripled to serve more people. . . .

CHAPATI
makes 4 pieces
Ingredients
2 cups of whole wheat flour
1 teaspoon salt
Few drops of oil for frying

In a large mixing bowl, combine flour and salt and add about ¾ cup of water. Stir into a dough with a wooden spoon. Dough should be firm but not sticky so add a bit more flour if necessary. When well mixed, turn out onto a lightly floured board and knead about 5 minutes until smooth and pliable. Roll into a ball and cover with a damp towel and let dough rest 10 minutes. Divide dough into 4 balls and roll out into 6-inch circles about $1/8$ inch thick. Stack each piece between wax paper before frying. In a very lightly oiled frying pan over moderate heat, fry each chapati a few minutes on both sides until it becomes light brown with a few dark brown heat spots. Do not heat beyond a pliable stage. Stack finished chapatis under a towel to hold warmth until served.

Tips—At the table, diners tear the pliable chapatis into bite-size pieces to scoop up food, instead of using a Western utensil. A great way, perhaps, to get finicky youngsters to try new dishes. While it would be possible to spend several days on the trail in Khyber Pass country with a few chapatis in your pocket, unless you find it necessary to do that, eat them fresh. Note the reference to blending your own whole wheat flour in the Tip section of the following recipe.

A bread popular in East India is paratha, a cousin of the chapati, which can be made quite fancy or simply, as in this recipe. . . .

NEPALESE PARATHA BREAD
makes 8 pieces
Ingredients
2 cups of whole wheat flour
¼ teaspoon salt
2 tablespoons vegetable oil, approximately, for dough
extra oil for brushing tops and frying

In large bowl combine flour and salt. Slowly add oil, mixing with fork or dough blender utensil until mixture looks like fine bread crumbs. Slowly add about ½ cup of warm water, mixing into a firm dough with a wooden spoon and hand. Roll into a ball and cover with clear plastic wrap or damp cloth for 30 minutes. Knead dough until pliable, adding water if dry or flour if sticky. Divide dough into 8 balls. On lightly floured board, roll out each ball into a 4-inch circle. Brush tops with oil, dust very lightly with flour and fold in half. Brush tops with oil again, dust very lightly with flour and fold again into a flat triangle. Stretch and flatten by hand to form a very flat triangle. Lightly oil frying pan and on medium high heat, fry bread on each side, turning until bread turns a light golden brown with some dark brown heat spots. Add a little more oil to pan if necessary. Place bread on paper towels briefly to absorb any oil and place in covered dish to keep warm until served.

Tip—You can blend your own whole wheat flour by mixing well together a ratio of about 1½ cups of white all-purpose flour to about ½ cup of bran or breakfast bran flakes which have been finely ground in a bowl by rubbing the flakes repeatedly between the thumb and fingers of one hand. (Whole wheat flour is about 25 percent bran.)

The Queen's own Cuisine

Back in the Days of Empire with Mother England long weeks away by ship and with so many colonies around the world that the sun never set on the British flag, Hong Kong was about as far away from London as one could possibly get. Inhabited by pigtailed people with ever-so-curious ways, the newly-arrived British likely looked upon their role in this barren and isolated place as something akin to colonizing a distant planet. Or being banished to Australia.

Indeed, from the time the flag was first raised on the north shore of Hong Kong Island on January 26th 1841, nearly three decades passed before Queen Victoria in 1869—feeling the place had perchance become sufficiently civilized for a royal visit—dispatched her son, the Duke of Edinburgh, to check out the place.

Royal family visits over the ensuing years provided pageantry from time to time with plumed parades, ceremony and cornerstone-laying. Then in 1956 Queen Elizabeth II became the first reigning British monarch to actually come and take a look. The *South China Morning Post* saw it as "an event unique in Hong Kong history." Elizabeth liked the place so much she returned for a second visit in May of 1975.

There is much about Hong Kong to impress even a monarch and the Queen must surely have noted the position it enjoys as one of the world's outstanding centers of international cuisine. While memorable local dishes abound in every capital city of the region, in Hong Kong the excellent offerings from virtually every culture seem endless, along with copious quantities of British fare, something you don't see much of elsewhere around the China Seas, except in a former colonial hostelry such as the venerable Raffles Hotel in Singapore or Penang's E & O Hotel on the Straits of Malacca.

While Asian food is generally considered something of a mystery by Westerners, British food can be something of a mystery as well. Their culinary cryptography seems designed to keep the rest of the world from figuring out what it's all about. Stuff like bangers and mash (sausage and mashed potatoes), tiddy oggie (Cornish pasty, a beef and vegetable turnover from the mines of Cornwall), chips (French fries) and crisps (potato chips). The deeper you get into it the more you appreciate the rigors foreign students endure with the study of English as a second language. It brings to mind a sign I saw in a little shop north of Manila, "English Spoken—British and American."

Here's one to ponder. The British long were the foremost and most far-reaching in riding the world's trade winds. So how did they fail to take seriously the wondrous things the natives were plucking off shrubs and trees and tossing into the cook pot? How is it that the glorious dishes and spices which they encountered along the way have not become an integral part of British national tradition, with dishes more, well . . . exciting?

Among the few items which did trickle back were pickling spices, chutney, ketchup, tea and Worcestershire sauce, the latter having been created by two British pharmacists from a recipe brought from India. But that seems to be about it.

Perhaps a lack of enthusiasm for hunting and gathering native things had something to do with Captain Bligh's blighted *Bounty* endeavor to ship those blasted breadfruit plants from Tahiti to the Caribbean in the late 1700s?

Ever-patient British friends explain that the Old Colonials were motivated largely by trade. Protecting trade routes resulted in the expansion of Empire. Then, along comes the wife from London and the first thing to go was the petite sloe-eyed cooking girl, followed by her bags of curry powder and chilies.

Proper British households were established and traditions followed. What the natives were up to was not much of a concern unless they became restless. Asia in those days was a far different world from the one we find today, strolling through the ritzy air-conditioned hotels and shops.

Encyclopaedia Britannica says of food Britannic: "few seasonings or sauces detract from the natural flavor of foods." Indeed, on my first visit to London in 1954 I heeded the counsel of friends who'd been there and, for most meals, sought out something like a Greek or Italian restaurant where the fare was more familiar.

In British households, particularly in the countryside, travelers report a more memorable dining experience than what restaurants offer. In further defense of what the British themselves seem disinclined to defend, some years ago *Bon Appetit* magazine produced "The Surprise of Britain" special collector's edition proclaiming, "The big news out of Britain these days is that the cooking is wonderful." But then there are reports from London-based friends that the legendary and challenging Falstaffian British Breakfast has given way to fast foods. Dreadful. I cannot recall a single bad day I have ever experienced after tucking into, at home, a British pub breakfast of bangers, Heinz beans on toast and a steamed tomato.

Despite what foreigners may see as a reticence in the use of seasonings, the British are legendary masters of the gentle art of herb gardening and the subdued application of herbs in the kitchen.

There's a lot to be said for that.

You be the judge. Coming up is a sampling from each end of the culinary spectrum. From Windsor Castle's traditions to the corner pub where pub grub reigns in the form of simple, hearty dishes such as ploughman's lunch, baked beans on toast, chips, or mash and bangers.

First, straight from Elizabeth's kitchen, as it appears in *Mrs. McKee's Royal Cookery Book,* we have Cream of Peas Monaco, a delicate soup which could well have graced the banquet table at the governor's residence during a royal visit to Hong Kong. That's followed, from the other end of the spectrum, by the northern pub favorite, mushy peas, typical of the hearty fare one might expect at the Old China Hand Tavern in Wan Chai, Hong Kong's feisty old fleet district.

Don't look for mushy peas across the harbor in the lobby of Hong Kong's posh Peninsula Hotel at tea time. Or at any other time for that matter. The word is, they're held in proper disdain by folks from the south of England. And it's likely any southerners who might enjoy eating mushy peas would never let on, while exercising a modicum of caution to make sure no one ever caught them in the act. I understand that there has never been a recorded sighting of mushy peas in London's Mayfair.

But mushy peas are, after all, a country cousin, just a few ingredients away from Cream of Peas Monaco, and not much different from a particularly hearty split pea soup; the kind where your spoon can actually stand up in the bowl. . . .

CREAM OF PEAS MONACO

serves 4

Ingredients

1 pound fresh green garden peas

2 pints beef stock

½ pint double cream (heavy cream or heavy whipping cream)

freshly ground pepper, salt and pinch of granulated sugar to taste

1 ounce butter

Garnish

1 tablespoon chopped mint

1 tablespoon sweet red bell pepper cut in small pieces

Cook the peas in salted water. Strain and sieve. Add the peas to the hot beef stock together with the cream, sugar and pepper and salt to taste. Heat thoroughly but do not boil. Then remove the pan from the heat and whisk in the butter. Garnish with chopped mint and red pepper. Serve hot.

Tip—Her Majesty might not approve, but frozen green peas work just fine.

MUSHY PEAS

serves 4

Ingredients

1 cup dried split green peas, rinsed

2 tablespoons butter

½ teaspoon salt to taste

½ teaspoon pepper to taste

Soak peas in 4 cups of water overnight removing any that float. Over medium heat, bring peas to a boil in their soaking water. Reduce heat to low and simmer, stirring occasionally, until peas soften, about 1 hour. Drain, add butter, salt and pepper and mash lightly. Stir well and serve hot as a vegetable accompaniment to a regular meal or with pub grub, such as fish and chips or baked beans on toast.

A Cultural Crunch
Between Planes

Since our arrival in Hong Kong in the early 1960s, monumental technological advances have been achieved in international air travel. But it didn't get to be more fun.

Airports of the region in the old days seem light years away from the clutter and clatter of today's overcrowded, sprawling, security-conscious labyrinths, which too often seem convulsed in the throes of renovation or relocation.

It really wasn't all that long ago that pilots sat toward the back of the plane with a parachute, goggles and a good bladder as basic equipment and after dark they found their way to the airport by aiming for a revolving beacon which shot a long bright shaft of light across the night horizon. On the first commercial flights, the pilot sat behind a lone passenger.

Ocean cruises have long been promoted with the idea that "getting there is half the fun," but with the changes in air travel in recent years, no airline could get away with saying that now.

On the bright side, as more people travel farther and faster and the comfort level slips further, travelers in the decades ahead likely will look back with envy at the relative ease and tranquility of air travel as we endure it today. American humorist Ogden Nash hit the nail on the head when he said, "Progress might have been all right once but it has gone on too long."

Back before the 1970s air travelers dressed as if fate might place them unexpectedly next to a long-lost high school sweetheart or maybe someone who might offer them a better job. You never saw or sat next to anyone—as you do today—who looked as if they might have made a direct transfer from a freight train, having just eluded a pack of bloodhounds.

And international airports around the world didn't all look so much the same back then. For example, in the Far East it wasn't at all uncommon to have an occasional local gentlemen or two lounging in the waiting room, as they did at home, in pajamas or underwear. Flights were shorter, less wearing, and you would sometimes find yourself on a long international flight with the plane and its services almost entirely to yourself.

Our initial flight from Seattle to Hong Kong required a refueling stop at Honolulu, where passengers disembarked into a World War II-era Quonset hut. Arriving and departing through these little prefabricated metal huts was not uncommon at airports serving major cities in the Pacific and the China Seas in those days. The thing that set Honolulu apart was the fact passengers received a complimentary glass of pineapple juice on arrival. Our onward journey required another stop at Wake Island to refuel and stretch our legs and that was followed by yet another in Tokyo.

Pacific air travel of that era was a tremendous advance over the 1935 inaugural flight of the China Clipper to Manila from San Francisco. That took six days of island hopping, with overnight stops at Honolulu, Midway, Wake and Guam, landing and taking off on the water. Just over 90 feet long, with a cruising speed of 163 miles an hour, the first China Clipper carried 18 to 40 passengers and a crew of five. On our move to Asia, 30 years later, our Boeing 707 jet cruised at 600 miles an hour carrying 219 passengers.

Asia was more quaint and quiet in our early days there but things tended to be less efficient. The slower pace caused even simple circumstances to waffle off in the wrong direction altogether, a phenomenon typically resulting from poor communication. The Westerner who spoke some Chinese or Thai or

Vietnamese was a real rarity and many of the service people who spoke English weren't particularly good at it, typically having a vocabulary pretty much limited to their own line of work, as I found the time I was waiting for a flight at Hong Kong's old Kai Tak airport when I dropped into the restaurant and ordered a bowl of minestrone.

Kai Tak, by the way, was replaced in 1998 by a mega-airport constructed on a reclaimed island west of the city. The relocation resulted in Hong Kong's losing a title it had held for over 70 years—The World's Most Harrowing Airport. It had a single runway, jutting out into the harbor like the deck of an aircraft carrier. The approach was a narrow winding thread-the-needle route at rooftop level over the city. Always a jaw-clenching experience, in bad weather and typhoons it was just no fun at all. In my 30 years in Asia, I averaged a Kai Tak landing maybe once or twice every month. Reflecting back on Kai Tak I can honestly say that I was actually terrified only two times . . . takeoff and landing. I may have souvenired bits of upholstery under my fingernails.

China Hands were inclined to explain to traumatized first-time arrivals that the landing pattern was a navigational aid, enabling the pilot to read the street signs to find the airport. On the bright side, there was some comfort in knowing that on a Kai Tak approach, jet airline captains paid very, very close attention.

But, back to my bowl of minestrone.

I had earlier come to understand that quality of Western food in Asian airports in those days suggested strongly that customers weren't expected back. However, I'd found minestrone always to be a pretty safe call, never having had a bad bowl of it anywhere in the world, although no two cooks make it quite the same. You can make a pretty good pot of it by just cleaning out the refrigerator.

As it turned out, as often happens to the best laid plans of people traveling overseas, the waiter misunderstood my order. Or perhaps he thought I might prefer something else. In any event, instead of minestrone, he brought a bowl of mulligatawny soup. This spicy curried concoction is almost always found on Indian restaurant menus despite the fact India really isn't much into soup.

This must have something to do with the fact that Indian food is designed to be—and tastes better if—eaten with the fingers, sopped or pincered into flatbreads. Soup, unless near the consistency of stew, is hardly suited for this.

Indian friends tell me mulligatawny came onto the scene simply to indulge British officers during the days of the Raj, who insisted *gentlemen* start dinner with soup. British officers tell me it came from the Tamils in southern India, derived from their term for "pepper water."

Eyeing my bowl of mulligatawny and not knowing a single word of Cantonese in those days I deferred to the waiter's misunderstanding and resolved the problem by the time-tested travelers' technique of simply disregarding it. But I couldn't help wondering if I'd asked for a Bombay duck snack, might the waiter have brought dried salted fish. Possibly. Bombay duck *is* dried salted fish.

The mulligatawny was fine, which shouldn't be surprising considering India and Hong Kong were geopolitical first cousins during those historic, heady, halcyon Days of Empire.

If you happen to find yourself between flights in Hong Kong soon and are inclined to try your hand at ordering minestrone at the airport don't fret if it happens to turn out to be rather like this tasty rendition of the old British Raj favorite. . . .

MULLIGATAWNY
serves 4

Ingredients
1 clove garlic, peeled and sliced
¼ teaspoon cayenne
1 teaspoon ground turmeric
1 teaspoon freshly ground black pepper

½ teaspoon ground cumin

1-inch piece fresh ginger, peeled and finely chopped

1 teaspoon ground coriander seeds

1 bay leaf, stripped from the middle vein and crumbled into small pieces

2 tablespoons vegetable oil

3 tablespoons butter

1 medium round white or yellow onion, peeled and finely chopped

1 fresh green chili, thinly sliced

2 chicken thighs, skinned, boned and diced, reserving bones for soup

4 cups canned chicken broth

3 tablespoons lentils

2 tablespoons rice

salt to taste

Garnish

5 sprigs fresh coriander leaves, rinsed and chopped

Place first 9 ingredients in food processor, chopper or mortar and grind to a spice paste. Place butter, onion and green chili in large saucepan and stir over medium heat until onion becomes translucent. Add ground spice paste stirring constantly over medium heat about 3 minutes. Add chicken and bones and stir about 1 minute. Reduce heat to low, add chicken broth and stir in lentils. When soup returns to simmer, cover pan and simmer 25 minutes on lowest heat, stirring occasionally. Add rice, cover, and simmer another 20 minutes, stirring occasionally until lentils are just tender. Remove bones and bay leaf. Add salt. Garnish with just-rinsed and chopped coriander. Serve hot.

Tip—This makes a nice first course for the Gurkha dishes mentioned in "This Food isn't for Sissies."

Putting Some Mussel into It

Along with the other truly momentous experiences in life we tend to recall the very first time we were persuaded to cinch up our most firm resolve and actually eat our very first garden snail. Despite the earlier years of disinclination, for many people that first bite has something of a potato chip appeal and they find it hard to stop after just one.

Then there's *bêche-de-mer,* the French term for the blobby sea slug which turns up in Asian soups, due in large part to the Chinese superstition that it makes a man more manly. If you have eaten sea slug you likely do not recall your very first time, as you were unaware that this was that gloopy thing in the soup and you really didn't want to inquire.

The subject of *bêche-de-mer* came up during a luncheon chat with Bernard Vigneau, owner of Hong Kong's popular Au Trou Normand restaurant shortly before he sold it and returned to France in the 1980s.

Asked how he prepares the dish Bernard responded firmly, "We French do not eat *bêche-de-mer."*

"Are you sure, Bernard?"

"I'm a French chef. I own a French restaurant. Believe me, we do not eat *bêche-de-mer."*

"But you've got a name for it."

"So do the English but they don't eat it either."

Another giant leap forward for cross-cultural understanding.

Bernard was one of those affable restaurateurs from the old school who roam casually around tables to chat with customers and make sure everything is as it should be. Despite the delightful lightness of Bernard's offerings, at the Au Trou Normand one did run the risk of overshooting the runway by overindulging while underestimating the voltage of his premium Normandy Calvados apple brandy.

Regulars kept an eye on the calendar to be sure to catch Thursday's ambrosian luncheon feature, mussels in white wine. The mussels arrived fresh that morning by air from France and it was essential to be on hand early for lunch as the supply was usually depleted minutes after 12 noon.

While mussels enjoy great popularity in a variety of delightful renditions throughout the China Seas, if you'd like to see why Bernard's offering was a particular favorite in Hong Kong, here's how to enjoy that dish at home. . . .

MUSSELS IN WHITE WINE

serves 4

Ingredients

¼ cup butter

1 clove garlic, peeled and chopped or passed through a garlic press

6 spring onions, rinsed, with roots and top few inches of green tops trimmed off and discarded, finely sliced

¼ cup dry white wine

⅓ bay leaf

2 pounds fresh mussels, rinsed and beards removed

salt and freshly ground pepper to taste

Garnish

2 tablespoons fresh parsley or dill, chopped

In a small saucepan, sauté garlic and onions over low heat in butter, stirring occasionally until onions are translucent. Set aside. In a large pot, simmer wine and bay leaf 2 minutes. Add mussels, the onions and garlic, cover tightly and increase heat to lively simmer. Occasionally agitate pan tightly closed, vigorously for more even cooking, just up to the point that mussels open, about 7 minutes. Remove from heat discarding bay leaf and any unopened mussels. Pour remaining mussels, along with the wine sauce, into heated serving bowls. Add salt and pepper. Garnish with parsley or dill. Serve immediately.

Tips—As with any seafood, the fresher the mussels the better. If you have trouble finding them they are usually available on special order at supermarkets. If you carry them home in a plastic bag, open it, as mussels must breathe and when you get them home put them in the refrigerator in an open container. In rinsing, expect to reject some, discarding any with cracked shells, which requires close inspection. Discard any which do not close tightly within a few minutes after tapping them and rinsing under cold running water. Hold each shell between the thumb and forefinger and try to move the two shells apart, applying only about as much pressure as you'd need in shelling a peanut. The two shell sections of a live mussel hold tightly together. Discard mussels with a shell which moves freely. Shells which have a little play in them may tighten up properly if rinsed again and allowed to rest a few minutes. Scrape off the little black beard with the edge of a sharp knife, and if you wish, any little barnacles on the shell too. Mussels cluster in great colonies on rocks along our Oregon coast, but we eat only those commercially cultivated and marketed under strict health controls. Mussels filter their food out of the water and, in view of some of the icky stuff in our oceans today, particularly near the shore, a wild mussel is something we would consider eating only if cooked to the texture of a fire hose.

Jimmy's Secret Recipe

There has never been another place quite like Old Hong Kong and it's unlikely the world will ever see anything quite like it again. Was the old girl as grand as she seemed? Indeed so. To know her was to love her. And it was possible—just hearing about her—to be smitten by her charms.

Asia Hand and author James Clavell held that Asia is "the center of the world, with Hong Kong the nucleus." Rather like a science-fiction robot capable of rewiring its own inner workings, Hong Kong has had a long history of reinventing herself every few years just to stay ahead of the game. In the early 1970s one of the major new cottage industries on Cheung Chau Island was "American Indian" beadwork for the US souvenir market.

In the early weeks of 1964 when we arrived in Hong Kong the population was roughly half of today's seven-plus million and this cozy outpost of Mother England gave no hint of the crunch which lay ahead. No one seemed particularly hurried. Bright red rickshaws skittered about all over town. By the 1990s only a little covey of them remained with their geriatric rickshaw "boys" at the Star Ferry, to provide photo opportunities for tourists.

In the 1960s the traditional pajama outfit or long robe with black cloth shoes remained in fashion. Shapely young ladies wore the bright, tight, slit-to-the-thigh *cheongsam*. Aside from those on display in touristy tailor shops, about the only *cheongsams* you saw in Hong Kong by the 1990s were those worn by hotel and restaurant staff, for tourists who expect to see that sort of thing.

Architecturally, Old Hong Kong has pretty much disappeared under the jackhammer and wrecking ball in recent decades but not all has been in the name of the dual demons of profit and progress. Just a few years ago the Hong Kong Buildings Department was receiving an average of three reports a day of bits and pieces crumbling off old buildings, which had to be torn down. Crossing the harbor on the Star Ferry today, it's something of a challenge to spot buildings which remain from just a few decades ago. It became increasingly common in the 1980s to set out for a favorite restaurant only to find that the relatively new 20-story building in which it was located had been torn down to make way for a newer 30-story building.

In the 1960s tourists had a limited choice of international hotels and sightseeing attractions. A "must see" in those days was the Lok Ma Chau border police station where you could peer into the hazy distance across the paddies and marshes into what was then known ominously as Red China.

Lok Ma Chau still draws some foreign tourists but if you want a quick look at China from Hong Kong today an air-conditioned tourist bus will zip you across the border for an afternoon guided tour of new urban sprawls which look about the same as Hong Kong.

Shopping and dining have long been among Hong Kong's major attractions and on our arrival I dutifully found my way to the highly-recommended Jimmy's Kitchen—after acquiring a top quality tailor-made tuxedo with cummerbund and tie, a white dinner jacket, two suits and two custom made shirts with two free ties thrown in. Total cost, well under US$150. When I last checked at a top quality tailor shop on the way to Jimmy's, that wouldn't get you a really first-rate blazer.

In those early days Jimmy's was located on Theatre Lane behind the old China Building, exuding an architectural ambience which former *Far Eastern Economic Review* editor Derek Davies described as "the dark polished wood alcoves and brassware of a London chophouse, a Paris brasserie or a New York steak house."

Unlike many restaurants in tourist centers, the place has remained something of a legend, retaining its high standards since opening in 1928. It was patterned after a Jimmy's Kitchen in Shanghai which was owned by a friend of Aaron "Jimmy" Landau, the founder of the Hong Kong edition. In 1993 the company published a hardcover compendium of 40 recipes titled *Jimmy's Secrets From Hong Kong's Best-Loved "Kitchen."*

I was disappointed, because the book did not reveal the secret of Jimmy's internationally-acclaimed pickled onions. A bowl of these crisp complimentary appetizers sets the taste buds to tingling.

Perhaps anticipating that the omission would disappoint many old-timers the book explains that founder Jimmy Landau created the recipe 50 years ago and the family has refused to divulge it "even to *Gourmet Magazine* of New York." That being the case I figured that the chance of their divulging it to me was pretty much out of the question.

But we don't have to let it go at that. I figured that if you could trace the DNA of that dish you would find a genetic link with traditional Chinese pickled onions. So I talked with Chinese friends and food industry officials in Hong Kong and Shanghai, and by juggling their "a little of this . . . some of that" and "a few days" or "a few weeks" a basic formula began to emerge.

Good cooks don't overdo so it's safe to surmise that whatever Jimmy's secret ingredient is, you don't need much of it and it had to be something which appealed to an Old China Hand. Thus, two teaspoons of good Scotch were added. While the code may not be completely broken, I like to think I got pretty close, particularly if you take into account a likely second secret ingredient: patience. These onions really begin to come into their prime if you can hold off for six weeks. Keep them near the front of the fridge and give them an occasional swirl from time to time while they're working.

One crunchy bite of these little guys causes visions of Jimmy's memorable menu to dance in my head. . . .

PICKLED ONIONS
Ingredients
15 walnut-size white pearl onions, root trimmed off with sharp knife

1 tablespoon non-iodized pickling salt

1 cup white vinegar

2 tablespoons sugar

12 black peppercorns

4 cloves

¼ bay leaf

⅛ teaspoon crushed red pepper flakes

1 piece fresh ginger, 1½ inches long, peeled, sliced into quarters across the grain, scored

2 teaspoons good Scotch

Bring a stainless steel or enamel pot of water, sufficient to just cover onions, to a boil. Add onions and when water returns to a boil, cover and boil no more than 2 minutes. Drain immediately and immerse onions in ice water, drain again and peel outer layer carefully with a very sharp knife and place onions in medium-size glass jar, in which boiling water has just been swirled about and discarded. Sprinkle salt over them. Cover jar with clear plastic wrap, secured with a rubber band. Set aside and swirl onions gently from time to time in juice which will accumulate. After 24 hours at room temperature, add cold water to just cover onions, swirl water one time, drain off and discard water, retaining onions in jar. Meanwhile, in a stainless steel or enamel pot, combine the vinegar, sugar, peppercorns, cloves, bay leaf, red pepper flakes and ginger. Bring to a boil, remove from heat and set aside to cool to room temperature. Pour over onions and add Scotch. Cover with plastic wrap, secured with a rubber band, and swirl onions a few times. Refrigerate for 6 or more weeks, swirling occasionally. You may use a shorter brining time, but the longer brine affords a mellower bite. Serve cold as an appetizer or party snack. In the unlikely event of leftovers, refrigerate them.

Tips—Due to the acidity, always use only glass or stainless steel for brining and pickling and a stainless steel or enamelware pot for boiling. Use wooden spoons to stir or lift onions. Use vinegar with a label indicating acidity of at least 5 percent.

The Parable of the Beggar

Returning home at the end of a long day it was good to know my wife would be there. Eventually that is, as her arrival was invariably an hour or so after mine with her typical 12-hour days as assistant principal at Hong Kong International School. Happily, we never had any of this "Let's go out dancing" or, worse, "You never take me anywhere."

At the end of a day in Hong Kong—one of the world's busiest, most crowded and frenzied cities—there is nothing quite like a quiet evening at home. Besides, she often bounced in beaming with a story to brighten the end of the day, typically one reflecting the challenge of an enrollment of 2,100 youngsters representing 39 nationalities.

One evening, close to Easter, she trundled through the door with briefcases and groceries and announced that in one of her seven kindergartens the teacher was talking about the religious aspects of the holiday and asked, "Can anyone tell me what the Last Supper was?"

As the little folks stirred in their seats, staring wide-eyed at the ceiling and going through the motions of what five-year-olds do when treading the terrain of really serious contemplation, the teacher put the question to them again. "Does anyone have any idea what the Last Supper was?" A waggling hand shot up in the back of the room.

"Yes, Billy . . . can you tell the class what the Last Supper was?"

"Chicken!" Billy blurted triumphantly, setting off a nodding of heads as the others muttered to one another, "I knew that."

Sharing this reminiscence does present something of a challenge. That is, the Last Supper story should lead us into a popular chicken recipe which you could whip up at home or order if you were out on the town in Hong Kong. The problem is there are so *many* chicken recipes. Yuan Mei, the eighteenth-century gourmet poet, saw chicken as "one of the four heroes of the table" (along with pork, fish and duck). No other cuisine begins to match the myriad memorable things Chinese do with chicken. You might choose to have lemon chicken, drunken chicken, Sichuan chicken, two-flavor or three-flavor chicken, stewed chicken with golden needle, steamed chicken, strange-tasting chicken, Hunan smoked chicken, black chicken soup or whatever. The choices seem endless.

Old China Hands and gourmets tend to concur that one of the best is beggar's chicken. It's what they would likely choose to order for you if you were being hosted at a special dinner in Hong Kong. Rating this from one to a high of ten, this dish is a definite 10 on the Surly Water Buffalo scale. That's the number of buffalo it would take to drag me away from a properly prepared serving of it, moist and tender with the meat slipping off the bone. For newcomers and visitors the host relates the legend of how this dish found its way into Chinese haute cuisine.

"Once upon a time, you see, a beggar stole a chicken and having no pot to cook it, he stuffed it with some scraps of food, packed it in lotus leaves and mud from a nearby pond and put it in the fire. Later when he broke open the hardened mud he was delighted with the heavenly aroma and delicious meal he found inside. Thus the name, beggar's chicken." The beggar's good fortune illustrates what Chinese sages have been saying all along, that life's great pleasures are often found in the most simple things.

Some recipes actually call for the chicken to be encased in "pond mud," a questionable suggestion today given the number of mucky Ming Dynasty duck and carp ponds you see on backroads, rippling with tiny bubbles of swamp gas. Other recipes call for a layer of newspaper in the wrap. A quaint touch. I've enjoyed beggar's chicken wrapped in a variety of printed Asian languages but this isn't something I'd recommend without knowing more about what kind of chemicals go into the manufacture of paper and ink today.

Preparing this dish at home—perhaps the only way you'll encounter it done well outside Asia—you can dispense with packing it in mud, clay or newspaper and enrobe it in unleavened dough instead.

But there is an even better option. Testing my recipe with former Taipei neighbor and Asia Hand Marda Stoliar, owner of Oregon's International School of Baking, she suggested, "The best way to do beggar's chicken at home is not with clay or dough but by placing the leaf-wrapped chicken in a large Western clay cooking pot, Asian sand pot or Japanese oven-proof pot. The flavor is the same but juices are better retained, it's more moist and less work." Having lived and worked a number of years in Asia and with an international reputation of knowing what she is talking about, Marda is right on all counts. She also knows Paris well and the French do a dish along these very lines called *poulet en cocotte.*

In spite of the high esteem in which beggar's chicken is held, few Chinese cookbooks carry the recipe. It's one of those dishes which Chinese order on special occasion when dining out. It does involve a lot of preparation if done at home. But hot out of the oven, the first bite assures you it was well worth it.

Bypassing the business with the unleavened dough makes it even less work and when baked, the dough isn't eaten anyway.

But don't count on Marda's method catching on with tradition-bound Chinese who clearly relish relating to guests the story of the beggar and his mud covered chicken. . . .

BEGGAR'S CHICKEN
serves 4 to 6

Seasoning A
½ cup regular soy sauce

2-inch piece of fresh ginger, peeled, quartered and lightly smashed

3 spring onions, rinsed, with roots and top few inches of green tops trimmed off and discarded, finely chopped

1 garlic clove, peeled and coarsely chopped

2 teaspoons five spice powder

½ cup dry white wine

3 tablespoons vegetable oil

1 teaspoon salt

1 teaspoon ground white pepper

Seasoning B
1 teaspoon sugar

¼ cup Shao Xing wine or good dry sherry

Ingredients
1 teaspoon peanut oil for frying

½ cup ham, sliced into small bite-size pieces

½ cup (4-ounce can drained) sliced bamboo shoots

4 dried Chinese or shiitake mushrooms, soaked 20 minutes in warm water, stems trimmed off and discarded, sliced ¼ inch lengthwise, drained, water discarded

8 golden needle dried lily flowers, soaked 20 minutes in warm water and cut in half

1 medium dill pickle, sliced thin lengthwise

2 spring onions, rinsed, with roots and top few inches of green tops trimmed off and discarded, cut into 1-inch pieces

1-inch piece of fresh ginger, peeled, quartered and lightly smashed

1 garlic clove, peeled, cut in half and lightly smashed

3 dried lotus leaves, soaked at least 2 hours beforehand in water in a large roasting pan, half full of water, until softened. (Placing a few cups on leaves helps hold leaves under water)

1 whole chicken (about 4½ pounds) with any excess fat, excess neck skin and wing tips cut off and discarded

1¼ teaspoons each of salt and white ground pepper, combined for chicken rub

3 whole star anise or 24 broken star points

6 feet cotton string to tie up bundle

Accompaniment

2 cups cooked rice

Prepare Seasonings A and B in separate bowls. stirring B to dissolve sugar. Set bowls aside. Warm wok over medium high heat about 2 minutes until a drop of water falling onto it makes just one sizzling bounce. Add peanut oil and increase heat to high and when oil begins to shimmer and light haze (not smoke) begins to rise, stir-fry ham about 1 minute to heat through. Immediately add remaining ingredients, bamboo shoots, mushrooms, lily buds, pickle, onions, ginger and garlic and Seasonings A and B. When heat returns to light simmer, cook 2 minutes, stirring occasionally. Remove from heat and strain through a sieve, retaining combined ingredients and liquid in separate bowls and set them aside.

Remove softened lotus leaves from water, shaking off excess water, and arrange on a cookie sheet to form an open envelope, overlapping in the middle in a three-leaf clover shape to create a flat surface large enough to hold the chicken. Place chicken, breast side up, on the leaves as you would a box being wrapped for mailing. When combined ingredients are cool enough to handle, rub chicken inside and out with salt and pepper mixture. Stuff the chicken cavity loosely with combined ingredients by hand until full, close the skin flap over the cavity, tie the legs together with kitchen twine or white cotton string and arrange any leftover ingredients on and alongside the body and on the top of the wings and legs. Sprinkle star anise on the skin of the chicken. Wrap soaked and softened leaves around chicken, overlapping one by one (firmly but not overly tight) to make a secure package completely covering chicken and wind string around wrapped chicken twice from top to bottom and side to side. Tie in a bow knot.

Turn chicken over and place in clay pot, breast down. Use a Western-style clay roasting casserole with glazed inside, rather than an Asian clay pot or sandpot. Gently pour all the reserved Seasonings A and B liquid over the wrapped chicken. Cover and place in the bottom of cold oven. Turn oven to 350°F (175°C) and cook to an internal temperature of 180°F (80°C), about 2½ hours.

Remove chicken from oven and let it rest 15 minutes. Place it breast side up on a large serving platter. Retain liquids in a small pitcher for diners to pour over their chicken and rice. Bring to the table hot with a large serving spoon. The host or hostess, or, more traditionally, the guest of honor, with kitchen shears or scissors, immediately snips the string. The host or hostess then opens the leaves with chopsticks and then, with shears or scissors, cuts up along the breast bone and into some of the flesh to afford better access to the stuffing. Serve with hot white rice.

Tips—If you can't get smoked Yunnan ham, try the dense, rich, lean West-phalian, Black Forest or Smithfield from the supermarket. Lotus leaves are available in Asian food stores in dried form.

The Joy of Cooking Pork

The Chinese say, "Those who have seen little marvel much." It's the way things are when you travel far or move a long, long way from home. After about six months of getting settled into a new culture this can evolve into "cultural shock." At this stage we begin to take note of little things which somehow failed to catch our attention earlier—or which lay in ambush—when we were so awed by all the new sights, sounds, and smells that the subtleties simply slipped past unnoticed.

While at the far dark end of the curve cultural shock can have heavy adjustment ramifications and lead to nail-biting and sniffling, it's just as likely to appear in more mundane forms which we can later share with friends back home as something simply novel or even amusing.

On its brighter side there's the Hong Kong banquet circuit where new-comers will be properly awed with the selection, preparation, creativity, variety, flavor and amount of food. But it's only after attending quite a number of banquets that you become aware that there is almost always a dish or two which you and the other guests—even the Chinese—haven't seen before. And it will dawn on you that you don't have the same things being served in the same old way as you do on the Western banquet circuit where rubber chicken, mushy potatoes and greasy gravy appear so often you just know that the guy they're getting this stuff from is some kind of super salesman. The cuisine of Hong Kong offers so many choices that the chance of a menu being repeated is about as great as the likelihood of your beating the odds at Macau's Lisboa Casino on Friday the 13th.

That brings us to sweet and sour pork, one of the most popular and iconic selections in Overseas Chinese restaurants. Pigs were domesticated in China thousands of years ago and except for the Muslim enclaves of the north, pork is the most favored meat in China. And, with typical Chinese ingenuity and resolve, through the millennia they've come up with more ways to prepare more parts of a pig than you could imagine.

With Asia's many time-honored joys of pork, sweet and sour may not even cross the host's mind unless it's included to provide visitors with something familiar.

In Hong Kong, when hosting friends from the States, I'd be inclined to go for a less familiar sweet and sour dish, such as chicken, duck, fish, or whatever. Or, there are such delights as pork with perch and crab sauce, gold coin pork, and pork and noodle broth with shrimp; just a few of the virtually countless selections visitors aren't likely to come across back home.

One of our favorite pork dishes goes by the unassuming name of white pork. Sometimes appearing on the menu as garlic pork, or pork with garlic sauce or boiled pork, it's typical of the cuisine of some areas of the South China Coast and is another one of those dishes you probably won't find in restaurants outside Asia. Its long and widespread popularity has endured since it came down from the north as an imperial and festive dish of the Manchurians when they established the Qing Dynasty which ruled China from 1644 to 1911.

White pork was one of the many house specialties which lured us often to Hong Kong's popular Red Pepper restaurant, in Causeway Bay, just around the corner from my office. And if we ever failed to include it when ordering, someone in the group—or our regular waiter—was sure to suggest, "and white pork."

Traditionally made from a large shoulder cut, I find it easy and just as enjoyable to use a pork tenderloin.

A simple dish by Chinese food preparation standards, give it a try and see if you don't agree it should be as internationally well-known as the ubiquitous sweet and sour pork, which in restaurants outside China is often mediocre at best. . . .

WHITE PORK
serves 2 to 4

Ingredients

½ round white onion, well chopped

2-inch piece of ginger, peeled, cut in half and scored lightly

2 teaspoons Shao Xing wine or good dry sherry

1 pound boneless pork tenderloin

Sauce

2 medium garlic cloves, peeled, minced or passed through a garlic press

4 tablespoons regular soy sauce

1 teaspoon sesame oil

¼ teaspoon chili oil

Garnish

6 sprigs fresh coriander leaves, rinsed

Without adding pork, in a large pot, add water estimated at enough to just cover pork. Stir in onion, ginger and wine. Rinse pork, pat dry with paper towels, cut loin in half and add to pot. Heat water to a boil, reduce heat to a simmer, partially cover. Cook about 30 minutes, turning a few times, until done, when a test slice shows no pink meat. Remove pot from heat and leave pork in cooking liquid 5 minutes more. Remove meat, allow to cool. Cover with clear plastic wrap and set aside, discarding cooking liquid and solids. Mix four sauce items together well in a bowl.

Slice pork as thin as possible, with your sharpest knife, into pieces about
an eighth of an inch thick. Arrange slices on a large serving plate in an
overlapping circular pattern. Drizzle sauce evenly in a thin circular ribbon
pattern, with some sauce on every piece. Garnish the outer edge of the
dish with coriander and serve at room temperature.

Tips—To check pork for doneness, make a test slice at its thickest part, down
to the center of the meat. Juice should run clear and meat should show no
pink. Traditionally, the pork is sliced "paper thin" but you should have no
problem slicing it to an acceptable fineness if you place the pork in the freezer
for 30 minutes and then with your sharpest knife carefully carve it. Let it return
to room temperature before serving. If you find you need a bit more sauce,
you can quickly whip some up by mixing 1 or 2 tablespoons of soy sauce to ½
teaspoon of sesame oil.

The Best Ribs in Town

One of the most momentous events in the history of Hong Kong occurred in 1984 when British Prime Minister Margaret Thatcher called on Beijing to discuss the 1997 expiration of Britain's 99-year lease on the New Territories, a buffer area which lay between China and the original colony of Hong Kong.

Hong Kong business interests—largely the ones with ties to Britain—had actively encouraged the dialogue, hoping an extension of the lease could be negotiated. Without it, the little enclave's boundaries would be pushed back, deep into the city, reducing British Hong Kong to little more than a hangnail on the long arm of China.

To the surprise of those who didn't fully grasp how the Chinese had always felt about what they called "the three unequal treaties" on which British Hong Kong was based, Beijing cordially advised Mrs. Thatcher that China was taking back the New Territories.

Oh, and by the way, the rest of Hong Kong as well.

Faced with the geopolitical realities, Britannia waived the rules and went along with the Chinese position, in spite of the fact it ran contrary to the British view that Hong Kong had been granted to Britain "in perpetuity."

The Queen's best diplomatic and political minds and her capable cadre of Old China Hands had anguished and reflected long and hard for an answer as to how Britain might get a better deal. But rather like Humpty Dumpty, all the queen's horses and all the queen's men couldn't put British Hong Kong back together again.

Allowing even for the Chinese propensity for patience, many found it curious that the People's Republic didn't simply send out engraved invitations announcing they would hold a reception in Hong Kong's Peninsula Hotel at noon Tuesday to take back the whole of Hong Kong. Over a span of nearly 50 years, since the establishment of the People's Republic, China had never recognized the old post-Opium Wars treaties anyway. To them, these Hong Kong treaties simply didn't exist.

With the curtain slowly descending on British Hong Kong, despite the uncertainties and apprehensions in the years leading up to the 1997 deadline, resilient Hong Kong held its position as one of the most dynamic and envied economies in the world. There were changes taking place, of course, and one of the most subtle was a quiet demographic one, with young scrubbed well-educated people, mainly in their twenties, moving in from America, the United Kingdom and elsewhere to fill a void created by the departure of young Hong Kong Chinese who had taken leave, to return later with a passport which afforded the family an emergency "parachute." Hong Kong had traditionally been a senior posting for international old boys. Any Western young adults were almost sure to be kids home from college for the holidays. Now, young Westerners were coming on their own, in pursuit of the golden dragon.

A couple members of this new breed would typically start out sharing one of Hong Kong's US$1,000-a-month, old, modest and cramped walk-up flats next to a noisy freeway on a little side street with a kitchen not much larger than a bathtub. Dinner typically was taken standing in front of a wheezy little old refrigerator, beneath a dim bulb which dangled from a cord from the ceiling. But they had caught the scent of the dragon and it was not unusual for those who held to it a few years—and caught its tail—to do very well indeed.

It was a particularly fortuitous era. At its height, daughters Heidi and Lesli met and married handsome, ambitious and promising young Americans, Oliver Silsby and Jerry Hammerschmidt, with the Lovely Charlene and I eventually acquiring eight more grandchildren, all born in historic Matilda

Hospital on Victoria Peak, high above Hong Kong. The sons-in-law, both in the investment field, would later observe that they could have saved money if—when they first got married—they had simply built a wing on the hospital's maternity ward.

Among this young breed of entrepreneurs were some who opened night spots and eateries, catering to Hong Kong's new, upbeat international customers. Among the more trendy and popular places were those which featured pork spareribs. Smart marketing, as ribs are popular in many cultures in both Asia and the West.

However, the question of how best to prepare ribs has caused as much impassioned debate among aficionados as chili recipes inspire among its disciples. It can be argued that some of the best ribs are prepared by the Chinese, who've likely been eating them since long before anybody else figured out how to catch and cook a pig.

In the early 1990s, Hong Kong's *Sunday Morning Post Magazine* sponsored "The Great Rib Round Up" to establish where "the best ribs in town" could be found.

Reporting on the surprising results of the contest, the article suggested that "not since Adam and Eve has a rib caused such controversy." It went on to speculate that the outcome "perhaps hinted at something most of us have always suspected about connoisseurship."

What happened was that the panel of international food experts, after a blind taste test, bypassed Hong Kong's most highly-hyped and trendy rib restaurants and awarded top honors to a rack of fast food shop ribs which had been slipped into the competition as a joke. The magazine noted the winning ribs sold for "about a quarter of the price of any of the other contenders and are served with one tenth the fuss." Lead Judge Martin Yan, international television chef and food writer, observed pragmatically, "Oh well, it's only a bit of fun, hey."

The winning ribs came from Maxim's Food Group which, at the time, was operating from nearly 300 locations throughout Hong Kong. This included

53 Chinese restaurants (some of palatial opulence), 18 European restaurants, 118 cake shops and 77 fast food and express outlets. Maxim's was serving some 320,000 people every day.

Maxim's senior manager Pierre Tang, a longtime friend and one of Hong Kong's most accommodating gentlemen, understandably stopped short of sharing their rib recipe, but, when asked, confirmed that the following guesstimate affords us a close shot at it. . . .

CHINESE PORK SPARERIBS
serves 4

Marinade

1 teaspoon garlic, peeled and minced or passed through a garlic press

1 teaspoon fresh ginger, peeled and minced or grated

1 tablespoon Shao Xing wine or good dry sherry

3 tablespoons honey

3 tablespoons hoisin sauce

1 tablespoon black bean garlic sauce

2 tablespoons regular soy sauce

1 teaspoon five spice powder

1 tablespoon sugar

Ingredient

Baby back pork rib bones, 5 or 6 per person. Have the butcher cut the rack in half lengthwise. Rinse and dry with paper towels. When cooked and ready to serve, slice racks into individual ribs.

Glaze

3 tablespoons honey

2 tablespoons hot water

Retained marinade

Combine marinade ingredients in a medium bowl, mix well and pour into large sealable plastic bag. Place ribs in the plastic bag, eliminating as much air as possible. Swirl bag to coat ribs evenly. Marinate at room temperature for 3 hours or in the refrigerator up to 8 hours, swirling bag occasionally. Preheat oven to 425°F (220°C). Fill baking pan ⅓ full with hot water. Place oiled wire baking rack over pan. Remove ribs from plastic bag, retaining marinade, and place ribs on oiled baking rack with space between pieces. Pour marinade into a medium bowl and mix well with glaze ingredients and set aside. Place pan with the ribs in oven on lowest rack. Bake about 10 minutes. Baste glaze on ribs. Turn ribs over, baste and bake about 10 more minutes. Check water level and add more hot water if pan is boiling dry. Baste. Turn and baste and bake about 8 to 10 more minutes. Check for doneness with a test slice between bones. Juice should run clean. Move pan with ribs to upper rack 6 inches under broiler and broil about 2 minutes. Remove ribs from oven, immediately slice into individual pieces. Place on serving dish and serve hot.

Well worth the effort, this great recipe—from China Hand and longtime friend and former neighbor Marda Stoliar—does involve a bit of work. However, if you are inclined toward an outdoor barbecue version of these cut-in-half ribs, here's how:

Prepare marinade, retaining 4 tablespoons for basting on the grill later. Marinate the ribs 2–3 hours. Preheat oven to 225°F (110°C). Lightly oil a baking pan and line with aluminum foil for easier cleanup. Remove ribs from marinade and place ribs in the oiled and foiled pan and cover pan lightly with a sheet of aluminum foil. Discard the used, saving the unused, marinade. Place ribs in the middle of the preheated oven, 2 hours. With the leftover unused marinade, prepare the glaze recipe. After the 2 hours in the oven, remove ribs, place on heated barbecue grill and baste the marinade on the ribs on the grill, 5 minutes on each side on medium heat. Remove ribs from grill and slice into individual pieces between bones before serving. Juice should run clear, indicating ribs are done.

An excellent main dish, just a few ribs are well-suited as a side dish. In ordering, keep in mind that "ribs" to a butcher tends to come across as a rack or a slab or a side of ribs so be sure the butcher understands that you want just a few bones. In eating these ribs, you can pluck them off the serving plate with a serving spoon or chopsticks, but this is one of those things best eaten with the fingers. Provide diners with a chilled moist washcloth. Also provide a bowl for bones. A bowl of warm black tea with a few thin slices of lemon may also be provided to clean and freshen fingers after eating. You'll find a ginger grater at an Asian market or a kitchen specialty shop. Ginger is stringy and when grating, little stringy nests may gather which should be removed with a toothpick and discarded.

Christianity, Cannon and Custard

Hong Kong, the best deep-water port between Yokohama and Singapore, might well have become a Portuguese colony if the Portuguese had been better received and if nearby Macau had not offered such an attractive alternative.

Additionally, officials in Canton rather liked the idea of the protection afforded by Portuguese ships and the superiority of Portuguese cannon at the mouth of the Pearl River.

A notorious pirate haunt even before the British arrived, it has been suggested that it is this pirate heritage which gave rise—over the past century and a half—to Hong Kong's free-wheeling dragon-eat-dog economic system which in some ways has operated more like a pit of vipers than an Austrian pastry shop.

Hong Kong history did not start with the British, despite the dismissive description of it by Lord Palmerston in 1841, who referred to it as "a barren rock with hardly a house upon it." Hong Kong has been inhabited for at least 5,000 years, and it's been established that people there were part of a cultural network stretching from Southern Taiwan along the South China Coast to Indochina 3,000 to 4,000 years ago.

It was in the early 1500s that the Portuguese became the first Westerners to arrive. Claiming to be paying tribute to the Ming Emperor, they hung around for seven years before being expelled in 1521. In the mid-1500s a verbal trade agreement was reached with Canton and Portuguese Macau was established, though it wasn't until 1887 that Portugal's sovereignty over Macau was formally recognized by treaty. Under the Portuguese, Macau became one of the richest cities in the world and was for centuries the hub of Asian trade with the rest of the world.

When the British finally showed up in the early 19th Century and asked local fishermen the name of the island, the Chinese, thinking the British meant the nearby village, replied "Heung Gong" which translates as "Fragrant Harbor," from the sandalwood incense made there. But it didn't take long for the smell of money to take over.

Victoria Harbour continues to afford one of the most spectacular panoramas in the world, either by night or by day, despite landfill having shrunk its grandeur to what critics say makes it more like a river.

The British arrived in Hong Kong in 1816 and after they declared sovereignty and settled in in the 1840s, Hong Kong's influence skyrocketed while Macau's plummeted. However, the early history written in that part of the world by Portuguese explorers, traders, priests and administrators is indelible. Among other things, they brought Christianity, cannon technology, and custard.

Custard has become so popular it's long been considered a native food. Prepared as a tart, it's a feature of proper *dim sum* breakfasts in Hong Kong. Even people who aren't much into sweets rarely allow the tart cart to pass without taking a few.

If you're unfamiliar with either of the following two naturalized Asian favorites, and perhaps curious to see how well custard blends with Asian cuisine, give them a try. . . .

EGG TARTS

makes 12 tarts

Pastry dough

1 cup all-purpose flour

½ teaspoon salt

⅓ cup and 1 tablespoon solid vegetable shortening

1 to 2 tablespoons ice water

Filling

¼ cup boiling water

2 tablespoons granulated sugar

6 egg yolks

¾ teaspoon vanilla extract

¼ cup regular whipping cream

Combine flour and salt in a large mixing bowl. Cut shortening well into flour mixture using a pastry blender utensil or a fork until it looks like tiny dry bread crumbs. If it seems overly sticky, cut in an additional tablespoon or two of flour. Stir in ice water 1 tablespoon at a time until flour is moistened through and can be easily gathered into a dough ball. Flatten into a circle on floured surface. Roll out to just under ⅛ inch thickness. Refer to Tip section on muffin tin. With a round 2½-inch cookie cutter, cut dough into circles and press them very lightly into, and up to the top of the rim of the cup leaving a slight lip. Place on cookie sheet and set aside. Preheat oven to 325°F (165°C).

Pour boiling water into a medium pot and add sugar, swirling it a moment to completely dissolve and cool. Add egg yolks, vanilla and cream to cooled sugar water and stir gently with a whisk until well blended, but without any bubbles. Strain through a fine sieve to remove any egg white.

With a soup spoon, ladle custard mixture into pastry shells not quite full. Place in the middle of the oven on the cookie sheet. Bake until custard is not quite firm at its center, about 20 minutes until a few crusts are starting to take on a bit of light brown color. Remove from oven and place muffin tin on wire rack. The hot custard will continue to cook a few minutes after it is removed from the oven and it is done when the tip of a toothpick, inserted into its center, comes out clean. After about another 20 minutes, very gently with fingertips, slightly rotate tarts a quarter turn to just loosen them from the tin. After another 10 or so minutes, after shells have firmed up a bit, with fingertips and a thin snippet of flexible plastic, work the tarts gently out and into your palm. Cover tarts with plastic wrap and refrigerate if you are not serving them within 2 hours to keep them from drying out. Serve warm or chilled.

Tips—Tarts sometimes stick to the tin. It seems to be a question of experience, your tin and your choice of shortening. I use a 12-cup mini aluminized steel muffin tin, with a high no-stick rating. From a specialty kitchen shop. It works fine ungreased or with a little butter or a solid vegetable shortening or a light misting of non-stick baking pan release spray. Whatever you use, apply it very lightly and if it gathers up a bit in the bottom of a cup, wipe it up with a clean cloth. Sprinkle a bit of flour very lightly over dough while rolling it out to keep it from sticking to the rolling pin. Just a little, as too much flour toughens the dough. Cut as many circles as possible from the initial rolling as handling of dough also toughens it. If a dough round tears, press it very lightly into the tart shell to repair it, or if there is an unduly thin spot patch it with a dampened bit of dough on your fingertips. Overcooking toughens custard. If you have uncooked custard left over, cook it along with the tarts, in a small oven-proof bowl.

*　　*　　*　　*

A popular first cousin to the Cantonese egg tart is the Philippine leche flan. Both share the same Spanish/Portuguese culinary legacy and—like its cousin—flan has been naturalized and is now considered a native dish.

In Manila, flan has been described as "tasting like falling in love. . . ."

LECHE FLAN
serves 6
Ingredients
1 cup canned evaporated milk
1 cup canned sweetened condensed milk
10 egg yolks
1 teaspoon vanilla extract
Caramel
1 cup granulated sugar

In a large bowl combine milk, egg yolks and vanilla and stir gently with a whisk, avoiding bubbles or foam, until well blended. Pour slowly into a large bowl through a fine sieve. Set aside.

Swirl sugar evenly in small heavy-bottom saucepan, creating a fairly level surface. Slowly and gently add ¼ cup of water. Do not stir. Turn heat to high to bring to a boil. Do not stir. When water boils, reduce heat to medium high. Do not stir. At this time, turn oven to 325°F (165°C). After about 9 minutes of boiling on the stove without stirring, mixture will begin to take on a light amber color. Pour *immediately* into a warm round

9-inch oven-proof glass or regular flan pan, such as a pie pan, about 1 ¼ inch deep, swirling to coat the bottom. Gently add the milk, egg and vanilla mixture. Put baking dish in a large shallow pan filled ¾ full with warm water and place in the oven on the middle shelf of preheated oven. Bake until flan is not quite firm at its center, about 40 to 45 minutes. Remove from oven, place baking dish on wire rack, and allow flan to cool to room temperature. The hot flan will continue to cook for a few minutes after it is removed from the oven and it is done when the tip of a toothpick, inserted into its center, comes out clean. Cover the cooled mixture with plastic wrap and refrigerate at least 5 to 8 hours before serving. To remove from cold baking dish, run warm knife carefully around sides of baking dish to loosen. Place serving plate on top of baking dish and holding both tightly together, quickly invert with a light shake and serve cold.

Tips—Cooling the flan in the refrigerator 5 to 8 hours will maximize saturation of caramel, enhancing flavor and texture. To clean any hardened caramel from a utensil, as soon as it is empty, pour boiling water over the caramel.

Steamed, Drunken and Dancing Shrimp

Chinese cooks came up with clay cooking vessels during the New Stone Age and the idea of steaming food must surely have occurred back around then when someone learned what steam does to your thumb if it gets in the way.

Since those distant days, the Chinese have learned to steam just about anything they could get their hands on—chicken, seafood, vegetables, bean curd, custard, fish, duck, dumplings, pork buns, beef, bread and goodness knows what all else.

This versatile, tasty, and healthy style of cooking somehow never caught on in other countries to the extent it did in China. Aside from hugging the cook, which should be done at least once a day, there is hardly anything you can do in the kitchen that's easier and requires less clean up. (See the "Woks and Steamers" section of the *Chef's Notes,* page 18.)

While steaming is one of the best ways to protect a food's flavor and texture, it also brings out the very best in things which live in water. But, Western cookbooks, aside from those dealing with healthy eating, rarely give it a nod, which perhaps would strike a Chinese as one of the many Mysteries of the West, along with the question of why we would choose to bake bread rather than frying or steaming it as they do.

In Hong Kong, steamed shrimp are often served unshelled with the head on. It creates a relaxed and fun atmosphere if diners peel their shrimp at the table and slosh the little guys into the sauce or dip with their fingers.

I've always been somewhat in awe of Chinese friends who have mastered the skill of chopsticking an unshelled shrimp into their mouth and neatly peeling it through some mystical unseen application of tongue and teeth. The shell is ejected with the crisp efficiency of a returning Automatic Teller Machine card. One of those techniques perhaps not meant to be mastered by foreigners, it would clearly intimidate the heck out of guests at the table if you could ever get it right. After years of trying to figure out how it's done, I've succeeded only in putting a remarkable amount of roughage through my system.

As noted in the Tip section of earlier finger food recipes, when serving things such as unpeeled shrimp it is customary to place on the table a large finger bowl containing warm black tea with a few thin slices of lemon in it which removes the shrimpy scent from fingers. It is also standard procedure to have a moist, chilled washcloth alongside the guest's plate.

Sauce or dip is served with steamed shrimp in little side dishes and the choice of sauce varies from one restaurant or region to another. Bottled soy sauce on the table is pretty much a Western aberration. Even a moderately qualified Chinese cook, operating out of anything above a backstreet food cart, would take some offense at diners presuming to improve on his or her dishes by squirting soy sauce onto them. The dipping sauce which is brought to the table with a particular dish is *the* sauce which has been prepared for *that* dish. Although there is no rule which says you can't also use the crab dip for your shrimp or pork if you so choose.

Seafood sauces and dips are most likely to contain some blend of soy, sesame oil, ginger, chilies or garlic, with maybe some chopped fresh coriander or spring onion. Perhaps you'll detect a bit of mild local vinegar or wine or fish sauce or a few drops of fresh lime or lemon or a splash of water.

Varying these ingredients in almost any reasonable manner will produce a sauce which is sure to be very much like something you'd find today somewhere around the China Seas. Or if you prefer, simply serve soy sauce in a little side dish. Adding a bit of Worcestershire to the soy sauce does wonders for an egg roll or its little brother, the spring roll.

Seafood in Hong Kong, both in its preparation and freshness, is among the best in the entire world. As one might expect, since the sea is just a short hike from anywhere in the territory. At home there, if we weren't doing shrimp Chinese style we would on occasion snack on large shrimp with a dip of plain mayonnaise served with a wedge of lemon. That's how take-out prawns from San Francisco's Fisherman's Wharf were eaten hot out of the huge sidewalk cook pots, when I lived just around the corner in the early 1940s. Then, a quarter's worth of prawns was about as much as a teenager could eat.

For a steaming plate of shrimp, or cold crab, it's hard to beat the Thai dip *zap,* which may also be spelled *zaap* or *saap.* Or some other way. With five tones, 48 vowels and diphthongs and assorted other challenges, the Thai language doesn't yield easily to being rendered into a standard Western written form. To further confuse things, this word trickled across the jungled border from Laos as *saep,* translating as "very delicious." A Thai may tell you "zap" means "spicy" which to them *is* "very delicious." While the name sounds rather like a faulty light switch zinging your finger, you can turn the heat down on this without losing its flair by using less chili or adding a little cold water.

Any one of the following dips, enough for one pound of steamed shrimp, adapts well to slight variations to suit your taste and the ingredients are easily adjusted upward or downward for more or fewer guests. . . .

THAI ZAP SAUCE
serves 4

Ingredients

1 teaspoon fresh garlic, peeled, finely chopped or passed through a garlic press

1 teaspoon fresh Thai chili, finely chopped

2½ teaspoons fresh coriander leaves, rinsed and finely chopped

2½ teaspoons spring onion, finely chopped

2 teaspoons lime (or lemon) juice

1½ tablespoons fish sauce

2 teaspoons cider vinegar

1 teaspoon water (optional)

Tip—Thai chili, red or green, is short and slightly curved like a lady's little finger at tea.

One of the more typical Chinese seafood sauces, which you will encounter in homes, restaurants and at food stalls all over Hong Kong and the China Seas, is the following quick combination. . . .

VINEGAR AND GINGER SAUCE
serves 6

Ingredients

¼ cup apple cider vinegar

4 tablespoons fresh ginger, peeled and minced

5 fresh coriander leaves, rinsed and finely chopped

One variation, popular along the coastline of South Asia, displaces the ginger with a prudent amount of small, thinly-sliced chilies. Or, chili sauce or chili garlic sauce from an Asian market may be served alongside other dips. Another great sauce is the zippy dip which Hong Kong Noodle King Harry Wong puts together when he drops by for a visit.

As an accompaniment to hot or chilled cracked crab or shrimp, Harry's dip carries our taste buds and conversation right back to the old days in Hong Kong when he was our neighbor high in the rolling green hills over Deep Water Bay. . . .

HARRY WONG'S SAUCE
serves 6

Ingredients

4 tablespoons apple cider vinegar

3 tablespoons red wine vinegar or red rice vinegar

2 tablespoons regular soy sauce

few drops fresh lemon juice, to taste

salt to taste

On an early visit to Shanghai, a short distance upriver I encountered a shrimp dish coated in a heavy brown gravy-of-sorts which overwhelmed the shrimp, once again endorsing the axiom that the less one does to shrimp or crab, the better. Asking around, I learned that the gravy was a typical embellishment along that stretch of coast around Fuzhou. Called "red cooking," it involves soy sauce blended with sugar, oil, ginger, tomato and spices and thickened with cornstarch.

One of the many variations on this theme is Fuzhou's famous red cooking paste, made from fermented red rice. It's typically used with fish and meat. In Hong Kong, Guangdong, Shanghai, and to the north, red cooking likely will involve braising fried meat or fish in soy sauce and brown sugar.

When it comes to doing something different and memorable with seafood, drunken shrimp is one of the more unusual delicacies you are likely to come across. It works something like this. Live shrimp are brought to your table and they're given a brief dip in wine or some volatile local liquor for a quick bit of revelry and jumping about. Then they're briefly boiled alive and served hot with a special sauce, typical of that region. Delicious.

In other parts of the world, you may come across some spinoff version, using raw shrimp which may be grilled, streamed, boiled, fried, in a *sushi* roll or soup, or whatever. And there's a *seviche* rendition with the shrimp "cooked" in lime juice. Basically, in the Asian version they are cooked alive after a brief boozy dip.

Could you possibly have shrimp fresher than that? Oh, yes. Indeed.

There's *dancing* shrimp, a unique and memorable dish, which may sometimes appear on a menu as a variation of drunken shrimp, and there's some confusion and a lot of legend involving the two terms. But cooked drunken shrimp are a long way from what is known in Thailand and Taiwan as *real* dancing shrimp. This is in a class all its own, skipping the sissy cooking business altogether and eating the shrimp alive, jumping and kicking. Something like the 1930s American college craze of swallowing live gold fish.

I stumbled onto dancing shrimp on an early trip down the west coast of Taiwan with Chinese friends who were working on the idea that if they kept at it long enough they might find some local culinary oddity I couldn't deal with. They never did but, in the eight years I headquartered in Taipei, they never gave up. Though they almost got me the night they introduced me to smoked sheep brains.

Reflecting back on the encounter, I've wondered if they call it dancing shrimp because of the way the shrimp splish-splash erratically about in the wine, or because of their particularly unruly behavior in your stomach for days after you've eaten them. They just can't seem to stop dancing and it's this unsettling afterglow which makes it difficult to harbor any feelings of sympathy for the barbarically dispatched crustaceans.

Considering the many delightful ways you may come across something called "drunken" or "dancing" shrimp, before you order it, ask how it's cooked. If they look puzzled and ask what you mean, you may want to consider opting for something else.

Or make it at home, such as our recipe which is about as close as you can expect to get to the real thing without a ready source of tiny live shrimp. . . .

DRUNKEN SHRIMP
serves 2 to 4
Ingredient
1 pound large shelled shrimp
Marinade
½ cup Shao Xing wine or good dry sherry
1 teaspoon regular soy sauce
1 medium garlic clove, minced or passed through a garlic grater
1-inch piece of fresh ginger, peeled and cut into 6 coins
Oil
½ cup peanut oil for frying
Garnish
4 sprigs of fresh rinsed coriander

Accompaniment
Thai zap sauce (page 184)
roasted pepper salt (page 248)

In a large bowl add shrimp to well mixed marinade and set aside ½ hour
at room temperature, stirring gently occasionally. Remove shrimp with
slotted spoon, discard marinade and drain shrimp in colander 5 minutes.
Warm wok over medium high heat about 2 minutes until a drop of water
falling onto it makes just one sizzling bounce. Add oil and increase heat to
high and when oil begins to shimmer and light haze (not smoke) begins to
rise, add shrimp and stir-fry just enough to heat shrimp through, about 2
minutes. Remove shrimp to serving plate, garnish rim with sprigs of
coriander and serve hot with sauce and pepper salt alongside in small soy
sauce dishes.

Names that Give One Pause

If you spend much time in and around China you'll experience a number of fancy, whimsically-named dishes which are virtually unknown in the West.

One of the most popular is Buddha Jumps Over the Wall, a culinary ensemble which is so delicious and memorable it's suggested the vegetarian Buddha would jump over a wall to get at it.

A Cantonese creation which may include as many as 30 ingredients, it's not likely you'd find any two chefs agreeing on exactly what those ingredients are. Pork has been a major ingredient the times I've come across it. It's labor-intensive and ingredients are so debatable, it's unlikely you'll find it in a cookbook as authors are disinclined to suggest that *this* is how to make it.

Another oddly-named favorite is the Sichuan dish, Ants Up the Tree, which involves neither ants nor a tree. The basic ingredients are minced pork and translucent bean thread vermicelli noodles which, when cooked, look something like ants on twigs. Our old friend from Taiwan days, China Hand Barbara Williams, calls this her "absolutely favorite" Chinese dish.

And whenever we think of Barbara it brings to mind the story of her first day on the job with the Joint US Military Assistance Group in Taipei in the early 1970s. She was single and her maiden name was Way. Having just arrived, Miss Way was unaware that the Chinese telephone greeting is *"wei"* which is pronounced the same as her name.

Everything went fine that morning until she answered the phone:

"*Wei!*" said the caller.

"Yes," Barbara replied.

"*Wei?*"

"*Speaking.*"

"*Wei?*"

"This *is* Way!"

"*Wei. . . ?*"

"Sheesh!"

Aside from that, she had a pretty good first day on the job.

Here's Barbara's recipe for her "absolutely favorite" Chinese dish—with a heat scale we like—but feel free to cut back a bit on the heat, by reducing the *aka miso* or chili sauce. . . .

ANTS UP THE TREE

serves 2 to 4

Ingredients

¼ pound crinkly, translucent Chinese bean thread vermicelli noodles
(estimate amount from weight listed on package)

2 tablespoons peanut oil for frying

⅓ cup uncooked ground lean pork

1 spring onion, rinsed, with roots and top few inches of green tops trimmed off and discarded, coarsely chopped

1 tablespoon fresh ginger, peeled and minced

1 tablespoon Japanese aka miso hot red bean paste or Chinese chili sauce

salt to taste

Seasonings

1 tablespoon Shao Xing wine or good dry sherry

1 tablespoon regular soy sauce

1 cup chicken broth

1 ½ teaspoons red or green chili pepper with seeds removed, finely chopped
3 dried black Chinese or shiitake mushrooms, soaked 20 minutes in warm water, with stems trimmed off and discarded, lightly chopped

Soften noodles by placing them in a small mixing bowl of warm water 20 minutes, stirring 3 or 4 times, until pliable and soft to the bite. Drain and cut noodles into 3 to 4 inch lengths and set aside. In medium bowl mix together seasonings. Set aside. Warm wok over medium high heat about 2 minutes. Add oil and increase heat to high and when oil begins to shimmer and light haze (not smoke) begins to rise add pork and stir-fry until pork becomes gray. Immediately add onion, ginger and aka miso. Stir-fry until pork and ginger become red from the aka miso. Add the seasonings. Reduce heat, stir once and add noodles. Simmer and gently stir frequently until liquid cooks down, about 10 minutes. Salt to taste. Place in serving bowl and serve immediately.

Tip—Look for aka miso red bean paste in the refrigerator section of Asian food stores.

A Noodle in the Haystack

A popular dish we often encountered in restaurants in Taipei in the 1970s was an unassuming cold complimentary noodle appetizer. Made from soy beans, it had a nutty/sesame flavor with a firm bite and appeared to hang from the same family tree as the various Asian noodles which are fashioned from rice, wheat, buckwheat, potatoes, mung beans, cornstarch or yams.

The dish was called *gan sz,* which translates as dry silk. But learning more about it proved a major endeavor. People had trouble understanding what I was referring to when I brought it up from time to time.

My quest was complicated by the fact I was relatively new at this challenging tonal language which has 16 different words pronounced *"gan"* and another 29 which can sound something like *"gan"* to the foreign ear. And there are a total of 142 words pronounced *"chi, ji, zhi"* and *"xie"*—all of which, tumbled apprehensively off a foreign tongue, can sound like "sz." And that's even before you factor in the subtle tonal differences of the various dialects. The possible combinations of those nearly 200 Chinese words—listed in type this size— could maybe stretch the length of a half pound of untangled wet linguine.

Usually people eventually guess what I'm trying to say in Chinese. But for some reason this wasn't working this time.

Finally, I reached a point at which I decided to just run with my best shot. Except for one problem.

I couldn't find *gan sz* noodles. Whenever I inquired, shopkeepers had as much trouble as my Taiwanese friends in understanding. And I could never find it among the many varieties of noodles on the shelves.

Finally, tenacity was rewarded when I discovered I was looking in the wrong direction. Browsing one evening in one of my old cookbooks from Taiwan I came upon a color photo of a dish with the name Shredded Bean Curd Salad. It was the elusive *gan sz*.

It was another case of Chinese and Westerners looking at something and interpreting it quite differently.

To me, *gan sz* was a noodle dish.

To the Chinese, it was a salad.

Well, why not?

The Spring Festival is celebrated in mid-winter and the Chinese eat winter melon soup in the summer and fall. South China's succulent litchi nut is actually a fruit. They wear white at funerals. And a compass is a "point south needle." So, if they see *gan sz* as a salad, that's fine. I was just delighted to finally be on the right track.

Gan sz is made from the dried, shiny, ochre-colored skin which, during processing, forms on the surface of hot soybean curd milk. Rather than appearing in markets in the form of noodles, you'll find it either in sheet form or rolled up like a scroll in a clear cellophane package, labeled in English as "dried bean flour skin" or "dried bean curd skin" or "bean curd sticks" or "sheets." If you don't see it, ask a clerk for "dried tofu skin," or *foo pei* in Hong Kong. If that doesn't help keep looking around the shelves. But not in the noodle section.

An excellent appetizer, it may also be served as a main course by doubling up on the ingredients, to taste. . . .

GAN SZ

serves 2

Ingredients

1 teaspoon salt

¼ cup carrot, peeled and sliced into toothpick-size slivers, or thinly grated

¼ cup celery, strings removed, sliced into toothpick size slivers, plus 1 teaspoon celery leaves, lightly chopped

2 sheets dried bean curd skin, about 8 by 11 inches each

2 teaspoons salt

½ teaspoon baking soda

Seasoning

4 teaspoons sesame oil

1 teaspoon crushed red pepper flakes, or to taste

½ teaspoon salt or to taste

Garnish

6 sprigs fresh coriander leaves, rinsed, 4 lightly chopped, 2 unchopped for garnish

In a small bowl dissolve salt in 1 cup of water and add carrot slivers. Soak 10 minutes. Squeeze dry and set aside. In small saucepan bring 1 cup of water to a boil and add celery slivers. When water returns to a boil, cook 15 seconds, drain through a strainer and rinse in cold running water to stop cooking. Add carrot slivers to strainer, mix well with celery and set aside to drain. Place 1 bean curd skin on very wet paper towel and cover skin with second wet paper towel. Place second skin on top of that towel and cover second skin with another wet paper towel. After 10 to 12 minutes skins should be pliable. Separate skins from wet paper towels and cut each sheet into quarters for easier handling. Roll up each piece into a tube shape about 2 inches wide. Flatten tube slightly between your thumb and fingertips and with kitchen shears, or a knife, cut crosswise across the top into strips just under ⅛-inch thick and place loosely in a bowl. Repeat the rolling and cutting with the remaining sections. Set bowl aside.

Pour 3 cups of water into a large saucepan and bring to a low boil. Remove water from heat for a moment. Add salt. Add baking soda, slowly and carefully so it does not boil over. Return water to heat. When it returns to a boil add bean curd skin noodles all at once and stir gently for about 8 seconds until the color just begins to turn from ochre to white. Immediately remove from heat, drain through a strainer under cold running water a few seconds and plunge into bowl of ice water for a minute. When cold, gently fluff with wet fingers a few times and allow to drain through strainer 5 to 10 minutes. In a large bowl, add sesame oil and red pepper flakes and swirl gently to coat bottom of bowl. Add bean curd skin noodles with seasoning, carrots and celery and chopped coriander, gently mixing well, with wet fingers.

Cover with plastic wrap and set aside in the fridge for about 3 to 5 hours or more and salt to taste. Place on serving dish, garnish with unchopped coriander and serve chilled or at room temperature.

Tip—After retiring back to America, chatting with the owner of the Hunan Kitchen restaurant in our neighborhood, she said, "It is easier to do *gan sz,* and with good results, using regular Chinese egg noodles. The long white ones that look like spaghetti. Break them in half or into thirds and cook them the same as you would spaghetti and then follow the recipe and chill before serving." Chinese pragmatism again.

Cooked soy bean curd skin noodles should be soft but with a distinctly firm bite. Just a little overcooking will make them mushy. They should be moist but not overly oily. Dried bean curd skins are fragile. Larger broken pieces in the package may be softened with wet paper towels and sliced for use in *gan sz* while smaller pieces may be cooked briefly in soups or soaked until pliable and cooked with vegetable dishes.

As Easy as Duck Soup

During our years in Taipei we occasionally set aside an evening for the special treat of a visit to the Huei Bin Lou duck restaurant near the old city's historic West Gate. The restaurant had been famous for generations for their special regard for Peking duck and the flavorful utilization of the entire bird. It was one of those venerable old places, of which Chinese friends said, "You really get all of the duck, except the quack. And then they give you the bill."

Few tourists found their way to Taipei's outstanding little old eateries in those days; even those adventurous visitors who ventured beyond the coffee shop of their new international hotel. Such places often were tucked away up in the hills or on little lanes. When you know your way around a place there's an inclination to look upon that as a good thing. It follows that when one's favorite little old places are discovered by others, the ambience, tradition, service and food quality tend to tumble while prices risc. It's OK that *you* found the place. It just seems reasonable somehow that you should be the very last to know about it. An even more foreboding sign than a few newcomers is the appearance of a photo on the wall of the owner with a celebrity. That's a sure sign you'd best keep an eye out for a new little place.

One of the cardinal rules of travel is, when you want great food, simply find a particularly portly cab driver and ask him to drive you to his favorite eatery. It works like a charm. The first time we used that device, in the course of an Alaskan cruise, we found ourselves in a charming little old steak house in the hills above the harbor. The dinner was excellent.

In foreign climes it's not a problem if you can't read the menu, or the splotches on the waiter's apron. When asked for your order, you simply point out what looks good at the next table.

What if there are no other customers in the place? Easy. One day, driving up to Delphi from Athens—not knowing a single word of Greek—we ordered a great lunch in a tiny village eatery simply by wandering through the kitchen with our grinning waiter, pointing out a chicken here, a simmering soup pot there. The old unshaven cook, wearing an apron which, in itself, might have served as a menu of sorts, was delighted and really outdid himself.

But, we're getting away from the duck, one of China's earliest domesticated creatures, going back to sometime after the Peking man got the idea that there had to be an easier way to get dinner than to crash about in the woods and swamps in search of a nest.

Duck remains one of the most popular of all foods in China. Traveling China today, at almost every turn of a rural road you'll see anywhere from a duck or two in a mucky little pond to hundreds of them milling about in huge commercial duck farms.

In Taiwan, before it became so torn down, built up and industrialized, "duck cowboys" were a familiar sight in the countryside. It was sort of a feathered replay of the old cattle drives of the early American West. The way it worked was, a duck cowboy would acquire some ducklings and as the rice harvest started in the south, he would walk along with his flock as they waddled and nibbled their way north through the just-harvested fields. On reaching the city, the duck drover sold the fattened flock for a nice profit.

While palace and village kitchens throughout China have produced more ways to prepare duck than anyone else could ever imagine, Peking duck rules as the most favored of all renditions. Properly prepared, Peking duck involves gossamer wisps of spring onion, a dollop of tangy sweet bean sauce and a crispy bite of the duck's shiny succulent skin, all enrobed in an almost lighter-than-air crepe.

In real duck restaurants the rest of the duck then appears through the course of the dinner in a surprising variety of forms. The bones go into the pot in the creation of a hearty soup.

Generally, what is too often served these days in international hotels or upmarket restaurants is a haphazard mutant which involves a slab of meat and skin from a rather run-of-the-mill, ill-prepared duck, a crepe of sorts, chopped onion and some kind of sweet sauce.

That's maybe OK. The simple truth is, even when Chinese food isn't prepared quite right, it's still pretty good.

Anyway, in a touristy place, one really shouldn't expect to find the other bits and pieces of the bird appearing on the table with their own special application or with the bones rendered into a succulent soup as you would find in one of those grand old duck restaurants. That's perhaps just as well where Western tourists are involved as they probably would fret over what part of the duck might be coming next.

By the early 1990s with tourist travel into the mainland of China shifting into high gear, energized by a new revolutionary zeal directed toward making money, restaurants went to work mastering the nuances of attracting tourist dollars. Specialty, nostalgic, fancy, and theme restaurants began popping up.

During this innovative interim, in the course of a business trip to one of the provincial capitals with an associate, we were directed to a restaurant near the hotel where they served Peking duck. Though an old establishment, we found it had succumbed to modernization and had been tidied up and embellished. In ordering, we thought we'd misunderstood when the waiter asked, "Would you like to pick out your duck?" Well, it's not altogether unusual in the China Seas to pick out your live fish or snake and there are specialty restaurants in Singapore and Bangkok where you even select your uncooked vegetables as you would in a market.

But pick out our duck? We'd eaten our way through flocks of ducks over the years but this was the first time we'd been invited to pick a bird to our liking and had no idea of how one went about doing that.

Following our waiter to the plucked poultry department we made our selection. Waggling his upright thumb to assure us we'd chosen a "really number one" bird he scrawled a big number 171 across the duck's breast with a felt tip pen.

That struck a familiar chord. In my pre-Korean War days in Boise, as a reporter on *The Idaho Statesman,* the state prison was on my beat and at Thanksgiving I was presented a turkey with IDAHO STATE PRISON FARM stamped in large letters across the breast. The grim words seemed to loom even larger as the big bird emerged from the oven. The guests agreed it was the most memorable Thanksgiving turkey they'd ever seen.

Similarly, when Peking duck No. 171 was set before us that evening we could clearly read that we had, in fact, gotten the right duck. Happily, it turned out better than we expected in view of our being accustomed to having a specially-bred Peking duck prepared in a more traditional and unhurried manner. That would involve stitching up the cleaned bird, inflating it like a balloon, hanging it to air dry, applying seasonings and a boiling syrup and finally roasting it slowly in a special oven.

No. 171 had been hurriedly and unceremoniously deep-fat fried. It was pretty good but it fell short of the runway of being the real thing. If you want real Peking duck, you will have a better chance of finding it if you know a restaurant where it is a house specialty and it's a good sign if they require your ordering a day in advance.

You may have a cookbook with a recipe for Peking duck. There is only one thing to remember about preparing this special dish at home. And that is, don't attempt it unless you're a food professional or own a Chinese restaurant. It would be a rare Chinese housewife who would attempt the classic version at home. It's the sort of dish Chinese look forward to, when eating out. But when the mood hits at our house, visions of duck soup dance in my head and I zing the cleaver along the sharpening steel and dig out the old Chinese sand pot.

The first step in preparing duck soup, of course, is to find yourself a nice duck. Unless you live in an area where ducks are raised, you'll probably have to settle on frozen or partially frozen duck because that's how things are these days. On the plus side, you can find—in almost any Asian grocery—everything you need to transform your duck into a delightful authentic Chinese dish, on par with any you would find in a Hong Kong restaurant.

Having acquired your duck, at somewhere around four pounds, the next step is to get at its bones. That's the tough part, trying to decide which duck recipe to choose as the vehicle. The choices are legion.

For our purpose, let's turn to what is widely considered one of the best regional Chinese cuisines, Chiu Chow, from the coastal province of Guangdong just north of Hong Kong. This is one of those wonderful little enclaves where people manifest a particular pride in their region, heritage and—of course—their cooking.

Of Hong Kong's thousands of restaurants, one of the more highly-regarded by the Chinese was an old Chiu Chow place across from my office in Causeway Bay where they did things with young goose, pigeon and shark fin in a way that made you wish you could sit there and go on eating forever. It was one of those little places you'd likely walk right by and not notice if someone didn't point it out. The narrow entry was simply a little takeout with tantalizing cooked ducks and geese hanging in golden red splendor in the window. There was no English menu. The staff spoke only Chinese. Credit cards were not accepted. You'd rarely see a foreigner in the place and if you ever did it was quite possibly me. With the swirl and smoke of traffic and commerce just outside the door, it somehow managed to remain very much Old Hong Kong.

You won't find many aged-in-the-wood Chiu Chow places outside Hong Kong or Chiu Chow itself. But you needn't forego the pleasure. With the range of ingredients available at Asian food stores today you can do Chiu Chow at home.

This recipe, a variation of their popular preparation of young goose, calls for duck, which is more readily available and is an appetizing avenue toward those bones we'll need for the duck soup....

CHIU CHOW DUCK
serves 4 to 6
Ingredients

I duck, about 4 pounds with excess neck and body cavity skin removed and discarded, giblets retained for duck soup (next recipe)

½ cup Shao Xing wine or good dry sherry

I cup dark soy sauce

¾ cup regular soy sauce

3 tablespoons sugar

I teaspoon ground white pepper

3 spring onions, rinsed, roots and top few inches of green tops trimmed off and discarded, lightly chopped

2-inch piece of fresh ginger, peeled, cut into ½-inch coins

I piece of Chinese dried orange peel (the size of a medium potato chip) or ½ teaspoon fresh orange peel, grated

6 whole star anise or 48 broken single star points

2 cinnamon sticks

Sauce

I tablespoon peeled garlic, minced

4 tablespoons apple cider vinegar

Garnish

6 sprigs of fresh rinsed coriander leaves

Accompaniment

I cup hot rice per person

Place duck in pot with enough boiling water to just cover it. When water returns to a boil, reduce heat to a simmer, cover and cook duck for 6 minutes. Remove pot from heat. Remove duck and set aside, discarding liquid. Rinse pot and without yet adding duck, fill again with enough water sufficient to just cover duck. Add remaining ingredients to the liquid, return pot to heat, stir a few times and when it boils, reduce heat to a simmer. Return the duck to the pot and cook, covered, for 1 hour, occasionally stirring liquid, until duck is cooked through to the bone. Meanwhile, in a small bowl, combine garlic and vinegar and set aside. When duck is done, remove duck and set aside to cool. To test for doneness, make a test slice at the leg joint and if juices run clear it is ready. If so, discard liquid. Bone the cooled duck and with the skin on, slice into bite-size pieces, retaining the bones. (Any meat remaining on the bones will enhance the following duck soup recipe.) Place duck on serving dish with sprigs of coriander around the rim and serve at room temperature with the garlic/cider sauce in small soy sauce dishes with the hot rice alongside.

Tips—All Asian ingredients will be found in Asian food stores. In grating fresh orange peel do not grate down past the colored part.

*   *   *   *

A Chinese proverb with particular application in the kitchen is, "Good things take time."

That also happened to be the secret of my Swiss Granny's noodle soup. Served each Saturday as a family tradition, we youngsters looked forward to it with such anticipation that we tended to express the passage of weekdays in terms of how many remained until—or had passed since—Granny's noodle soup day. If we agreed we'd go swimming "the day after noodle soup day" it was understood this meant Sunday.

Granny's soup simmered slowly all morning on the stately old wood stove, filling her kitchen with savory sniffs which set us to salivating like a pack of Pavlovian poodles.

In the China Seas it's much the same. As author Amy Tan notes in *The Joy Luck Club,* "Chinese mothers show they love their children . . . with stern offerings of steamed dumplings, duck's gizzards, and crab." All patiently and properly prepared, of course. In the case of duck soup, give it at least an hour-and-a-half simmer to coax the flavor out of the bones.

Chinese restaurants generally make today's soup from yesterday's bones unless you are involved in one of those banquets which typically run over two hours.

The foregoing Chiu Chow Duck recipe, which provides the bones, is well-suited to accompany duck soup, as the duck is cooled, boned and served at room temperature, affording you plenty of time to prepare the soup. . . .

DUCK SOUP

serves 2 to 4

Ingredients

Bones of 1 duck (retained from foregoing recipe)

Giblets (retained from foregoing recipe), thinly sliced (except the neck)

¼ cup ham, cubed

3 tablespoons Shao Xing wine or good dry sherry

½-inch piece of fresh ginger, peeled, cut in half and lightly smashed or heavily scored with a knife

2 spring onions, rinsed, with root ends and top few inches of green tops

trimmed off and discarded, lightly chopped

½ cup cabbage leaves, chopped bite-size

⅓ large dill pickle, thinly sliced lengthwise

¼ teaspoon salt or to taste

3 ounces crinkly, translucent Chinese bean thread vermicelli noodles
(estimate amount from weight listed on package)

Garnish

1 tablespoon fresh rinsed coriander leaves, coarsely chopped

2 sprigs watercress, coarsely chopped (optional)

Add duck bones, giblets, ham, wine, ginger, onions, cabbage, and pickle to large soup pot with enough cold water to almost cover. Bring to a boil, reduce to a simmer, covered, for 1½ hours, stirring occasionally. Strain through a sieve, retaining liquid and other sieved ingredients while discarding bones and neck. Return liquid and ingredients to pot, salt to taste, return pot to stove over low heat, covered, to maintain warmth. Soften noodles by placing them in a small mixing bowl covered with warm water for 20 minutes, stirring 3 or 4 times, until pliable and soft to the bite. Drain and cut noodles into 3 to 4 inch lengths and add noodles to soup. Ladle soup into warm bowls. Add garnish to soup and serve hot.

Tips—All Asian ingredients called for will be found in Asian markets. For the ham, to get closer to China's distinctive smoked Yunnan ham, try the dense, rich, lean Westphalian, Black Forest or Smithfield from the supermarket.

The Duck Stops Here

Island hopping in the Philippines, one learns early in the game that an essential phrase for the heavily-hosted foreigner is *busog na busog,* which in the national language of Tagalog translates as "I'm really stuffed." Not only is Filipino hospitality legendary, so is their snacking. The Filipino snack is called *merienda.* It can be formidable and it can come at any time of the morning or the afternoon. And it usually does.

On my first trip into the provinces outside Manila, I braced for the journey with a larger-than-usual breakfast and at our first stop—about an hour later—found a gargantuan *merienda* laid out for us. At the next stop down the road we were ushered into yet another. We had four *meriendas* that morning before lunch and this scenario repeated after lunch until we arrived at our overnight stop for a filling and festive Filipino dinner.

A whole roast pig—sometimes a calf—was a frequent feature of lunch or dinner on these travels. It's the Filipino way of letting you know they're happy to see you. Visitors planning on prowling the provinces are advised to learn how to pace themselves through this munchy marathon. The secret is, take only a nibble of this and a nibble of that, with the frequent incantation, *busog na busog.*

Though not well-known internationally, Filipino food is distinctive, laced with splashes of vinegar and slices of garlic with an emphasis on rice, chicken, pork and seafood. It's a zesty mix of native, Chinese, Malay, American, Mexican and Spanish, the latter two dating back to the days of the galleon trade when Spanish influence literally traveled east and west from Spain in both directions around the world, meeting in a wonderful culinary melange in Manila.

One of the most popular dishes in the Philippines, with foreigners as well as Filipinos, is *adobo.* It also happens to be one of the more popular dishes in Hong Kong because at the time of this writing there are some 140,000 Filipinos living and working there. Filpinos had become, by far, the largest foreign community in Hong Kong.

Garlic is something of a staple in the Philippines and you'll note that the following recipe calls for an entire bulb, not just a single little clove. In Manila you can always tell when neighbors are about ready to sit down to dinner by the heady wisps of garlic riding the evening air.

If you've ever been lucky enough to experience a proper adobo anywhere in the Philippines it would have been made pretty much along these lines. . . .

PORK ADOBO
serves 4
Ingredients
2 pounds boneless pork, well rinsed, cut into bite-size pieces

1 entire bulb of garlic, individual cloves separated, peeled and lightly crushed

4 teaspoons regular soy sauce

1 teaspoon ground black pepper or whole peppercorns

½ cup white vinegar

1 teaspoon vegetable oil for frying
Accompaniment
4 cups hot cooked rice

Place all ingredients except the oil in large saucepan with 2 cups of water, bring to a boil and reduce heat to a low simmer, cover, and cook about 1 hour, stirring occasionally, until about 1 cup of liquid remains. Remove any foam which may form. Add more water if necessary to bring liquid up to about 1 cup. Remove from heat and remove garlic with a slotted spoon and set aside. Remove pork with slotted spoon and set aside. Pour liquid into a bowl, set aside and using the same large saucepan, fry garlic in oil, on medium heat 1 minute, stirring often. Add pork and fry on medium heat about 2 minutes, stirring often. Add ½ cup of retained liquid and simmer uncovered about 5 minutes, stirring occasionally. Transfer to the serving bowl and serve hot along with a serving bowl of hot rice. Place any remaining warm liquid on the table in a small pitcher for guests to add to their adobo if they wish.

Tips—Do not scorch garlic. This is a relatively moist dish and in the event you end up a little short on the liquid, you can extend it in a jiffy by simply heating and adding a little chicken bouillon. To serve eight, this recipe may be doubled. Adobo is also traditionally made with boneless skinned chicken or equal parts of chicken and pork.

*   *   *   *

Traveling throughout the Philippine archipelago, you'll find no food more startling and memorable than the *balut,* a cooked duck egg with a full-blown chick inside, just hours away from hatching. Few foreigners develop a taste for them. The eggs are sold at night, hot, by street vendors whose calls of *Baluuuuuuuut!* echo through back streets and barrios like the wail of an orphaned water buffalo. If you ever find yourself prevailed upon to try one, be advised they are best consumed in a dark corner, late in the evening, after several cocktails.

A major cottage industry, *balut* are typically made in a low unobtrusive structure of bamboo or thatch with a metal roof and dirt floor, where the fertilized eggs are incubated for 14 to 18 days in a pit packed with warm rice husks and then boiled for 20 to 30 minutes in a large wok-like pot.

In contrast, *ensaymada* is a sweet breakfast item consumed daily by the carload in the Philippines and makes an immediate hit with foreigners. Tracking down this recipe, I was somewhat surprised to find that—like noodles—it's something rarely made from scratch at home. And it is a rare Filipino domestic or housewife who knew how to make it, despite its popularity, which goes all the way back to the days the country was a colony of Spain. The reason for that is simple. Melt-in-your-mouth *ensaymadas,* baked in old wood-fired ovens, are available in even the most remote barrio bakeries.

Friends in the baking industry in Manila provided the recipe and while we don't much indulge in rich sweets, when I made this the other morning I topped it with a tiara of melted butter, grated cheddar and powdered sugar. The Lovely Charlene ate five and I had seven. . . .

ENSAYMADA
makes 12 rolls

Ingredients

3 cups all-purpose flour

½ teaspoon salt

1 tablespoon granulated sugar for yeast

1 tablespoon regular active dry yeast (see Tip section)

3 egg yolks, beaten with fork until smooth

2 tablespoons granulated sugar for dough

Vegetable oil, sufficient to lightly coat inside of sealable plastic bag for dough

1 tablespoon melted butter for brushing on dough

Topping

2 tablespoons melted butter for brushing on buns

2 cups cheddar cheese, finely grated

3 tablespoons powdered sugar

In large bowl mix flour and salt together and set aside. In small bowl mix together ½ cup tepid water with sugar and yeast, stir, and set aside until froth begins to appear on the surface, about 10 minutes. Add yeast mixture to flour and stir in egg yolks and second sugar ingredient with a wooden spoon until it can be turned out onto a lightly floured board and kneaded into an elastic dough, 8 to 10 minutes. Shape into a ball, lightly oil the inside of a 1 quart sealable plastic bag and place the dough inside and let it rest at room temperature 30 minutes. Remove dough from bag and roll it out into a large rectangle about 15 inches long and ¼ inch thick. Brush top with melted butter and roll it up tightly into a long cylinder. Cut into about 12 pieces, just over 1 inch thick. Place pieces down flat on a large greased baking sheet about 2½ inches apart and let rest 10 minutes. With palm, press and flatten each roll to about 1½ inches apart and let rest 10 minutes more. Flatten again to just over 1 inch apart. Let rest 30 minutes.

Bake in middle of pre-heated 375°F (190°C) oven until tops begin to change color and bottoms just begin to become golden brown, about 10 minutes. Remove from oven, place rolls on wire rack and brush immediately with melted butter, blanket lightly with cheese and dust with powdered sugar, through a fine sieve. Serve hot or cold.

Tips—Ensaymada may be served with butter or melted butter. Instead of the old standby active yeast, "rapid" or "instant" yeast may be used, but if so, blend it directly into the dry flour. Then add the water. I prefer active yeast, operating on the principle that if you are in a rush you likely aren't having much fun in the kitchen.

German Tourists' Favorite Fare

There are differences of opinion in Hong Kong as to which restaurant has the best Peking duck or who the best tailor is, but there is one thing about Hong Kong which everyone can agree on, and that is that there is no other place quite like it.

Friends who knew it intimately and those just passing through enthused over it as one of their favorite cities, the sort of place you could maybe live forever. Old Shanghai was "the Paris of the East" and its neighbor, Suzhou, with its canals, was seen as "Asia's Venice." But such comparisons seemed somehow out of place to those who really knew the territory.

A "borrowed place on borrowed time"—as it was called before the British reluctantly joined China in tossing aside the old imposed treaties, many of its roving band of international characters could have swaggered right out of the pages of Hemingway or Clavell.

One such cast member was Dr. Hans Dietrich, the head of the German diplomatic mission in Hong Kong in the early 1980s, who we met at dinner one evening in Kowloon. We had come by taxi, a more leisurely option than wrestling our car home along Hong Kong's bustling streets after a typically long and challenging day of trying to figure out what's going to happen next.

As diners dispersed at the end of the evening, Dr. Dietrich spotted us in the Peninsula Hotel taxi queue and offered us a ride. As we snaked along the dark, narrow jungled road overlooking Happy Valley, I commented on the comfort of his spiffy new car. With that easy subdued smile which all diplomats do rather well, he observed, "Also, tonight you have one of Hong Kong's better-paid drivers."

It wasn't until some time later that a mutual friend provided additional details about our soft-spoken and unassuming driver. Dr. Dietrich, the friend confided, was one of the youngest officers, and the captain's adjutant, on the legendary battleship *Graf Spee* when it went down in 1939 in the early days of World War II. During a long and devastating Atlantic raid on merchant shipping, the *Graf Spee* mistook three smaller and faster British ships as part of a convoy and was cornered in the neutral South American port of Montevideo. On Hitler's orders it made a final run for the sea where it was scuttled to keep its engineering and armament designs from falling into British hands.

But that's not the end of the story. Instead of sitting out the war safely in Uruguay, Dietrich escaped, crossed the Andes and, alone, made his way circuitously to Brazil, eventually catching an Italian plane back to Germany. Years later, D-Day caught him in the English Channel in command of a torpedo boat which hit a mine with the loss of 20 of its 28-man crew. He spent the rest of the war as a prisoner of war in the United States.

After the war, joining the diplomatic service, he was assigned to the mission in Wellington, where Dietrich met New Zealanders who'd helped put down the *Graf Spee*. And they made him an honorary member of their veterans' association.

It's said everyone's life is a novel. In Hong Kong, it often was a blockbuster novel.

Back when I first began basting my brain with ideas for this book, I wrote Dr. Dietrich in retirement in Germany and asked, "What special dish was served to dinner guests at your residence when you were Consul General in Hong Kong?"

"Always," he replied, "German visitors coming out of China asked if they could have *Eintopf!*"

This simple, substantial meal of peasant parentage is a classic old German favorite, as readily available in a village *Gasthaus* as it is in restaurants in Berlin or Munich. *Eintopf* is literally "one pot" and it's something of a national culinary treasure; a meal in itself, just as *pho* is to the Vietnamese or *sukiyaki* to the Japanese or stew to the Irish.

Eintopf appears in myriad forms—from savory soups to rich stews—and the hearty vegetable and sausage casserole which follows could well have been your main course if you'd had the pleasure of dining at Dr. Dietrich's residence in those days. . . .

EINTOPF

serves 4

Ingredients

¼ cup barley

¼ cup lentils

¼ cup green split dried peas

5 cups chicken stock, fresh, canned or bouillon cubes

2 large sprigs celery leaves, rinsed

½ teaspoon dried marjoram

½ teaspoon dried parsley

1 large potato, peeled and coarsely chopped

1 large carrot, peeled and coarsely chopped

1 medium celery rib, cut into ½-inch sections, rinsed

2 crisp medium leeks, roots and dark green part and first outer leaf trimmed off and discarded, rinsed well, sliced in half lengthwise, rinsed again and coarsely chopped

2 slices thick cut bacon, with excess fat trimmed off and discarded, finely chopped

¼ round white or yellow onion, finely chopped

2 cooked German beef or pork sausages, cut in half lengthwise and sliced
into ½-inch pieces

Accompaniment

French bread or rolls and a green salad

Rinse and drain together barley, lentils and peas. Bring chicken stock to a
boil and add barley, lentils, peas, celery leaves, marjoram and parsley.
When water returns to a boil, reduce heat to a simmer and cook 20
minutes, stirring occasionally. Add potato and carrot. Return to simmer
and cook 15 minutes, stirring occasionally. Add celery rib and leeks.
Return to simmer and cook 25 minutes, stirring occasionally. Meanwhile,
fry bacon in a pan until done. Remove bacon from pan and add onion and
sausage and fry until onion becomes translucent. Stir bacon, onion and
sausage into pot and simmer a few minutes. Serve hot.

Soup or a Salad?

The things which tourists and first-timers take for granted today when roaming around the world!

For example, salads in Asia. Now standard fare in tourist hotels and international restaurants throughout that part of the world, this has not long been the case. Western-style salad greens were pretty much avoided until things like California lettuce began arriving fresh by jet from halfway around the world in a matter of hours.

For a host of health reasons, eating local vegetables raw was avoided by Asians and Westerners alike. In those days, commercial chemical fertilizers had not yet come into vogue in that part of the world. Farmers did what they had done since the dawn of agriculture: generating their own organic natural fertilizer and sprinkling it on the vegetables. The tender-tummied among us had good reason to be cautious.

The problem was endemic and in some areas it was actually considered polite cocktail party parlance to discuss with the ambassador's wife the gurgly state of your gastroenteritis and whether tepid 7-Up and/or soda crackers might moderate a dysfunctional digestive system.

Drinking water was either boiled at home or commercially bottled. Anything eaten raw was first soaked in a bowl of water with an antiseptic. Everyone called it "pinky water" rather than potassium permanganate, a name which rolls off the tongue like a glob of cold peanut butter. If pinky water sounds unappetizing, there was the option of a half-hour in a mild bleach solution and then rinsing them in boiled water.

Living in Manila in the early 1960s we often took our salad in the form of *gazpacho,* the chilled Spanish vegetable soup which is now firmly entrenched as a traditional Filipino dish. This refreshing chilled uncooked soup is an Andalusian rendition of spring salad and is perfect for a casual and healthy light lunch on a hot day or for the start of a fancy banquet.

Friends in Manila shared with us their old family recipe, part of the country's legacy of the 400 years of Spanish rule. . . .

GAZPACHO
serves 8

Ingredients

1 garlic clove, peeled and coarsely chopped

1 medium round white or yellow onion, peeled and coarsely chopped

1 cucumber, peeled, seeded and coarsely chopped

3 tomatoes, peeled and coarsely chopped

1 green bell pepper, coarsely chopped

¼ cup vinegar

¾ cup tomato juice

salt to taste

Cayenne pepper to taste

¼ cup olive oil

Puree ingredients in blender or food processor. Taste for seasoning. Chill in refrigerator 4 hours. Serve cold.

Tips—For ease in peeling the tomatoes which go in the blender, first plunge them into boiling water for a minute and then into ice water. The degree of smoothness or chunkiness is a matter of personal choice. Look at it this way. It's your blender and your kitchen so don't allow yourself to be intimidated on this point. The Lovely Charlene purees *gazpacho* to a smooth paste and serves it along with small bowls of finely chopped green bell peppers, spring onions, cucumbers and unpeeled tomatoes, along with croutons. Diners add the garnish at the table to their taste.

*   *   *   *

It is easy to infer that salads are a big item in traditional Asian cuisine, judging from all the so-called "Asian salads" we run across in food magazines and trendy restaurants today. But that's not the case. These dishes spring from the imagination of creative Western chefs. Taste good and likely good for you. But not Asian. However, there is a particularly notable authentic Asian rendering of raw greens which is popular in Thailand. It's their beef mint salad. It's become a fairly regular menu item in overseas Thai restaurants. Once you've tried it, chances are you'll watch for it in the future.

Exploring the delights of Thai cuisine on my first visit to Bangkok in the early 1960s, I've been happily hooked on it from the very first fortuitous encounter. And, in recent years, it's been good to see it gaining a foothold in the West, with Thai restaurants springing up in places where folks had no idea of what they'd been missing.

A number of Asian dishes, such as *sushi, pho* and *kimchi*—which my Western generation never heard of growing up—have filtered into the American scene in recent years. In the mid-1940s my high school pals and I would wander a few blocks over the hill into San Francisco's Chinatown into one of the little old Cantonese chop suey eateries, where, slipping into one of the private curtained booths, we'd sprinkle an assortment of communal coins and a dollar bill or two on the table and, without looking at a menu, would simply say, "Bring us something *you* like to eat." We were never disappointed. And it was always more food than we could eat.

At this writing, our favorite San Francisco Chinatown restaurant—on Grant Avenue near California Street—is, we hear, the only one which still has the old-style curtained booths. Things change. But what hasn't changed is, when ordering in an Overseas Chinese restaurant, tell them to prepare your food the way the *cook* likes it. It makes a difference.

It wasn't until I got to Hong Kong that I came to understand that until fairly recent years, virtually all Chinese restaurants in America served a sort of Cantonese food—that is, something along the lines of Hong Kong style—because that is the region where the early Chinese immigrants had come from.

In recent decades, with a wider range of regional Chinese restaurants popping up here and there overseas, one of the earliest and most notable and immediately popular cuisines, on the American scene, was the hot and spicy food of Sichuan province. Hot on its heels was the introduction of spicy Thai and Vietnamese food and their acceptance was helped along by another factor. Just as American veterans returned from Europe after World War II with a taste for pizza and wines, thousands of servicemen on R&R from the Vietnam War discovered Thai food while savoring the many exotic delights of Bangkok.

If you've not yet come across beef mint salad, do yourself a favor and try my easy recipe for this zippy and refreshing dish which—while totally typical of tropical Thai cuisine—has what it takes to enhance almost any lunch or dinner. . . .

THAI BEEF MINT SALAD
serves 2

Ingredients

½ pound beef sirloin, sliced into strips 2 inches long, ¼ inch thick and ¼ inch wide

2 tablespoons fresh lime juice

1 tablespoon fresh lemon juice

1 teaspoon sugar

¾ ounce translucent Chinese bean thread vermicelli noodles, estimate amount from weight shown on package

3 spring onions, rinsed, with roots and top few inches of green tops trimmed off and discarded, coarsely chopped

1 cup fresh mint leaves, rinsed, stripped from stems

3 firm small tomatoes, cut into thin wedges

3-inch section of cucumber, peeled, sliced as thinly as possible

½ teaspoon fresh red Thai chili, finely chopped

¾ teaspoon salt, or to taste

Garnish: 2 sprigs fresh coriander leaves, rinsed and coarsely chopped

Fry beef over medium high heat until color changes, about 2 minutes. Set beef aside on paper towels on a plate and cool in refrigerator. In a small bowl, mix lime and lemon juice with sugar until it dissolves and set aside. Soften noodles by placing them in a small mixing bowl covered with warm water 20 minutes, stirring 3 or 4 times, until pliable and soft to the bite. Drain and cut noodles into lengths of 3 to 4 inches and set aside. In large bowl, mix remaining ingredients together, along with lime and lemon juice. Add cooled beef and noodles and mix well gently. Place in serving bowl. Add garnish and cover with plastic wrap and place in refrigerator to chill 2 hours before serving.

Tips—If you prefer this less hot, remove the seeds and white pith from the chili before chopping. And always wash hands well after handling chili as you'll be glad you did in the event you rub your eye with your finger, which for some reason, always seems to happen. Chiliholics may prefer to add a bit more chili with seeds or about $1/8$ teaspoon cayenne to taste. Mixing in a light sprinkle of curry powder adds a nice zip.

Sole Food

Perhaps we all carry in the back of our mind some questions which never seem important enough to clear up, simply by asking someone who knows the answer.

For example, in Hong Kong and Macau a menu will often list either Dover or Macau sole. What's the difference? Is "Dover sole" a style of cooking, a type of fish, or what?

I finally put the question to old friend Philip Mermod, then manager of the Hong Kong Hilton, and was assured that real Dover sole is fished in the English Channel and south of Dublin Bay and is considered the best of all flatfish. The Macau sole, fished around Hong Kong and Macau, is slightly shorter than its European cousin but is widely considered just as tasty if well prepared, Philip said.

Related to the flounder, Dover sole is exported frozen and may be found at better fish markets around the world. But much of what passes for Dover sole in America is really North American flounder, and there's much to be said for them. Much of the so-so sole in our local markets appears in small, thin fillets, sometimes so translucent you can almost read a newspaper through them, which makes it difficult to avoid overcooking or tearing. What can you do if this happens to you? Discuss it with your friend in the seafood section of your supermarket. In the event you're not on a first-name basis with someone there, *get* on a first-name basis and always exchange a pleasantry or two when passing by between purchases. It helps ensure that you always get what you want, in the freshest and firmest condition, along with a tip as to what is coming in next or when sales are coming up.

Sole appears on the menu in many different ways and the French, because that's how they are about food, have come up with 30 of them. If you were dining in Hong Kong or Macau this evening, you would likely find your Dover or Macau sole cooked in the classic *meunière* style, light and buttery with a sprinkling of chopped fresh parsley.

Sole is a particularly delicate link in the food chain and the less you do with it the better. It's one of those dishes prepared almost by instinct by a professional chef, with a flick of the wrist, but home cooks, with a little practice, can turn out a fillet as memorable as you'd hope to find on an evening out.

If you've never savored a real Dover sole at the old Hong Kong Hilton at sunset above the glittering harbor or a Macau sole on the verandah of Macau's colonial Hotel Bela Vista, overlooking the tree-lined sweep of the Praia Grande, this recipe will give you some idea of what it was like. . . .

SOLE MEUNIÈRE
serves 2

Ingredients

2 fresh sole fillets

salt to taste

pepper to taste

¼ cup all-purpose flour

2 tablespoons peanut oil

1 tablespoon unsalted butter

Sauce

2 tablespoons unsalted butter

Garnish
fresh parsley, chopped
2 lemon wedges

Pat fillets dry with paper towels and trim a bit from each end to fit skillet, if necessary. Salt and pepper each side and then lightly coat both sides with flour and shake off any excess. Set fillets aside on a dry plate. In a nonstick skillet large enough to hold both fillets, add oil and on medium-high heat swirl to cover bottom and heat until it begins to shimmer and a light haze, not smoke, begins to rise. Add butter and swirl to evenly coat bottom of skillet. After about 1 minute, when bubbling moderates, add both fillets and cook until edges begin to turn translucent and bottom is a golden brown, 2 to 3 minutes. Gently turn fillets (using two large spatulas to turn each one to help hold fillets together). After the second side has cooked about 1½ minutes test the top of the thickest part of the fillet with the tip of a knife and if it flakes easily it is done. Immediately place fillets on a warm serving dish and set aside. Pour off and discard oil from skillet and wipe well with paper towel. Add butter to skillet for the sauce with the heat on medium high, swirling lightly until butter melts. As soon as it begins to turn light brown, after about another minute, pour it evenly over the fillets. Sprinkle parsley over fillets and serve hot with lemon wedges.

Tips—To serve four, double this recipe, leaving the peanut oil at 2 tablespoons. Home cooks will have better luck with fillets of 5 to 6 ounces each, just under a half inch at the thickest part. Sole is easily overcooked so keep a close eye on it to assure that it has only a fleeting acquaintance with the medium high heat. Don't fiddle with fillets once they are in the skillet or lift them for a peek at their progress. Just put them in, turn once, and remove from the skillet when done. Until you've had a little practice, if it appears the heat is overly high you may want to lift the pan from the stove, from time to time, and swirl the oil a bit to avoid overcooking.

*   *   *   *

Fishing the bounty of Hong Kong and Macau waters for thousands of years, the Cantonese have developed an amazing array of wonderful ways to prepare their catch of the day. One of the lightest and most tasty is their rendition of steamed whole fish.

Fish dishes throughout much of Asia are traditionally prepared with the head and tail intact, but unless you have a sufficiently large steamer it may be necessary to remove and discard these. Western dinner guests—with their disinclination to look food in the eye—will likely be glad you did that. Traditional Asians, however, will perhaps wonder why you'd do such a curious thing, with the head being widely considered the most delicious part of the fish.

As a cultural footnote, in coastal areas of South Asia, it is considered bad luck to turn a fish on the serving plate, so diners work their chopsticks into the underside of the bone after the flesh is eaten from the top side. The superstition stems from the idea of a boat turning over and there are eateries along the South China Coast where you can almost hear the air being sucked in by the locals if a patron flips a fish on the serving plate.

When serving this dish at home, feel free to disregard the old superstition, unless you happen to have some Chinese fishermen as guests. . . .

CANTONESE STEAMED WHOLE FISH
serves 2 to 4

Ingredients

1 whole firm-fleshed white fish, about 1 pound

peanut oil for plate

1½ teaspoons Shao Xing wine or good dry sherry

¼ teaspoon ground white pepper

1 teaspoon peanut oil

1 tablespoon regular soy sauce

¼ cup of cooked ham, sliced very thin and sliced again into matchsticks

1 inch fresh ginger, peeled, sliced thin lengthwise and sliced again into matchsticks

3 spring onions, rinsed, with roots and top few inches of green tops trimmed off and discarded, cut in half crosswise and sliced lengthwise as thin as possible

Garnish

3 sprigs fresh coriander leaves, lightly chopped with stems removed, for fish

5 sprigs fresh rinsed coriander leaves

Rinse cleaned and scaled fish inside and out, pat dry with paper towel. With sharp knife, make half dozen quarter-inch deep diagonal cuts across fish on each side. Place fish on lightly oiled heat-proof dish. Mix wine and pepper in small bowl and rub lightly inside and on both sides of fish. Sprinkle top of fish with peanut oil and soy sauce and lightly rub in. Set aside for 15 minutes and then arrange half the ham, ginger and onion inside the fish and half on the top. Bring water in wok to a steamy boil. Place plate in a bamboo steamer large enough to afford sufficient space to allow steam to pass freely up to the fish. Cover and place steamer in wok, an inch or so over the surface of the boiling water. In 8 to 10 minutes pierce fish lightly with a fork. If it flakes easily to the bone it is done. Transfer fish to a warm serving plate with a wide spatula. Spoon some of the juice from the plate in which it was steamed over the fish. Sprinkle chopped coriander leaves over fish. Place whole coriander sprigs around the plate and serve hot.

Tip—Fillets of sole, or true cod, about a half pound per person, adapt well to this. To approximate smoked Yunnan ham, try a lean Westphalian, Black Forest or Smithfield from the supermarket.

When Feeling Crabby Try Thai

In preparing crab, there are a few exceptions to the old rule "the less you do to the crab, the better." One exceptional example is Singapore's remarkable rendering of stir-fried chili crab (page 103).

Equally memorable are the succulent crab claws, which in Thailand are cooked in a clay pot and go by the rather engaging name *kaam puu mor din,* which translates simply as "crab claw clay pot."

We often had it at home during our years in Asia and it remains a family favorite. As with an elephant round up, or being around people who smile all the time, this dish is a novelty outside Thailand. That is, unless you prepare it yourself. Happily, it is a quick and easy ensemble. A proper Thai clay pot may be hard to come by, but the Thai style is typically comfy, casual and friendly so simply use a standard Western pot or casserole—slightly larger than the crab—with a tight fitting lid, or a Chinese sand pot.

The partially-glazed clay *kaam puu* pot is basically a hefty version of the lighter sand pot which you'll find in Asian markets and works well for soup or seafood or curried Asian dishes. For *kaam puu,* be sure your pot has a sufficiently weighty tight-fitting lid, which is essential to keep the juice from escaping in clouds of steam during cooking.

When the dish is ready to be served, you should have about a half cup of juice in the bottom of the pot and this is typically spooned by diners over their accompanying rice and the crab as well.

Our *kaam puu* pot found its way into our home as a gift from a Thai friend, Bornchai Kunalai, as a token of his appreciation for my appreciation of Thai food. After nearly a half century of frequent use the old pot has survived six international moves, numerous major earthquakes and typhoons and it continues to occupy an honored, secure spot in our home.

Bornchai also shared favorite family recipes and if you enjoy Thai food, the following one for *kaam puu* could well become one of your seafood favorites. . . .

CLAY POT CRAB

serves 2 to 4

Ingredients

3 tablespoons bacon grease for bottom of pot or one slice thick bacon, chopped

4 leafy celery tops

3 dried black Chinese or shiitake mushrooms, soaked 20 minutes in warm water, cut in half with stems trimmed off and discarded

2-inch piece fresh ginger, peeled, sliced into 4 pieces

1½ tablespoons whole black peppercorns

4 tablespoons regular soy sauce

4 tablespoons Mekhong whiskey or light rum

2 tablespoons sesame oil

½ teaspoon salt

5 medium garlic cloves, peeled, quartered

3 spring onions, rinsed, with roots and top few inches of green tops trimmed off and discarded, unchopped

1 cooked Dungeness crab, about 1½ pounds, at room temperature, in the shell, cleaned, rinsed, claws and legs broken off and body cut into 6 pieces, lightly cracked

Garnish

4 sprigs fresh rinsed coriander leaves, lightly chopped

Accompaniment

1 cup of hot cooked rice per person

No water is added. Combine all ingredients, except the cooked crab, in a pot. Cover and cook on medium high heat for 15 minutes without lifting lid to better retain juice. Then quickly stir crab pieces into pot, generously spooning the juices over it. Cover and cook 5 more minutes on medium high heat without lifting lid. Serve hot in the cooking pot or turn out into a serving bowl, spooning juice over top and adding coriander garnish.

Tips—If using a freshly-killed uncooked crab, combine it with the other ingredients at the beginning and cook for 20 minutes, covered, without lifting lid for a peek. Set an empty bowl on the table for crab shells and provide each diner with a damp chilled washcloth. A bowl of warm black tea with a few thin slices of lemon may also be provided to clean and freshen fingers after eating.

Kimchiburgers and Sukiyaki Sandwiches

Westerners who spend much time barking their shins on the sharp corners of Asia's cultural nuances are inclined on occasion to quote Kipling's "East is East, and West is West, and never the twain shall meet."

But after three decades of shin-barking in the Far East, I have to go along with Asia Hand and author, Pierre Boulle, who opens his *Bridge on the River Kwai* with the lines, "The insuperable gap between East and West that exists in some eyes is perhaps nothing more than an optical illusion."

So was Kipling mistaken? He grew up in British India long before many Westerners ventured far or long behind the beaded curtain. That never-the-twain sound bite appears in the first two lines of *The Ballad of East and West*. But, hey, we've clearly missed what the Old Colonial was really saying. At the end of the poem, East and West do come together, with the lines: "But there is neither East nor West, Border, nor Breed, nor Birth. . . ."

Whenever I hear that never-the-twain business I take it as an opportunity for an exchange of views on how today's technological leaps in international travel and communications are bringing East and West together at a rate unparalleled in earlier times. And nowhere is that more apparent than in culinary circles. Pizzas and hamburgers are now virtual staples in places like Hong Kong and Singapore, while dishes from Bangkok and Saigon and Sichuan are gaining a wide following in the West.

Then there's this blending of cuisines, which has been going on since we first got up off all fours and started walking around, seeing what the other guys were eating.

Today this appears in some unlikely forms. *Sukiyaki* sandwiches for example, which I first encountered at an embassy reception. Served either hot or cold on soft dinner rolls, they were fantastic. And there is the Korean-conceived kimchiburger which calls for a hearty slurry of *kimchi,* an ancient form of pickled cabbage with—depending on the whim of the cook—a near-incendiary mix of garlic, radish and chili; a sort of sauerkraut with an engaging personality disorder.

My first encounter with *kimchi* occurred decades ago in the tiny old Korean Club Restaurant in Hong Kong's Causeway Bay theater district.

Described in the *South China Morning Post* as "not the kind of place to charm the pants off a client . . . but well worth a visit" the only outside indication a restaurant could be found on the fourth floor was a small sign in Chinese on the lobby mailbox.

I'd been shepherded to this up-and-out-of-the-way place by my old friend Marvin Farkas. A photographer and author, Marvin was something of a legend around Asia where, in a given week, his camera would swing from President Johnson in Manila, to US soldiers dodging incoming fire in Vietnam, to a covey of stunning models posing for an airline calendar in Singapore. Marvin's friends were never surprised to run into him anywhere from Madison County to an obscure noodle house somewhere in Thailand.

After our dinner that evening, stepping off the elevator which was barely large enough for us and two notably garlicky strangers, Marvin whispered, "The reason you rarely find a Korean restaurant above the fourth floor is because that's about as long as you can hold your breath in the elevator on the way down."

Babylonians are credited with being the first to come up with salted pickled foods around 1500 BC. Laborers on the Great Wall of China some 2,000 years ago relied heavily on shredded pickled cabbage in their diet. When the concept finally reached Germany it was adopted as the national dish, sauerkraut. Reflecting sound German logic, the name translates simply as "sour cabbage."

In Korea, pickled sour cabbage is more than a national dish. It's a national treasure.

If you ask a Korean how *kimchi* translates into English, they eye you rather curiously and reply, "Well, *kimchi* means . . . *kimchi*. Like, well . . . like spaghetti means spaghetti."

Appearing in 187 versions (according to Seoul's Kimchi Field Museum), it's served at virtually every meal in Korea and 15 cabbages is considered a fair average November-to-February supply of winter *kimchi* for one Korean. Served as a cold appetizer or accompaniment to a meal, it also appears in hot soup, stew and noodle dishes or it may be heated with sausage. Or whatever. Lightly chopped and cooked into your scrambled eggs? Why not?

As with cheap cigars and veterans' reunions, *kimchi* is not something widely popular with some Western ladies. OK. It isn't popular with *most* Western ladies. Its bouquet does tend to violate others' air space rather rudely. No one seems to be wishy-washy when it comes to *kimchi*. There's little middle ground. You love it or you don't. The Lovely Charlene tolerates my always having some around because she's convinced it keeps mice, moths and ants out of the house.

For wary US infantrymen in the Korean War, *kimchi* served something like radar, with some GIs claiming to be able to sniff out nearby Korean units from the wafts of garlic. A doctor friend tells of an associate who had an elderly patient who was in a coma and—after calling her name several times without any response—he leaned closer, tried again and the *kimchi* on his breath snapped her out of the coma. Really.

It's true that *kimchi* is traditionally stored in covered jars buried in the yard, providing you have a yard or live in the country. Today, the way things have changed in Korea in recent decades, urban apartment dwellers store their jars on balconies. That might upset a neighbor in Boston but in Korea it's OK as the neighbors do the same thing.

With the adoption of modern farming and marketing practices and the wide use of refrigerators, many Korean families—which previously prepared enough winter *kimchi* to last until spring—now keep only a small amount on hand in the fridge.

Returning home to Taipei from Hong Kong after my introduction to *kimchi* I chased down a recipe which—with tips from Korean friends and strangers—has undergone many modifications over the years, eventually evolving into one of the things you'll always find in our refrigerator alongside the sauerkraut and sourdough starter. The recipe is simple and the ingredients are easy to come by, a definite plus where *kimchi* is concerned as some variations call for everything from pickled corvina to sponge seaweed, whatever that is.

A Chinese would be inclined to see *kimchi* as a typical *bao tsai* or pickled vegetable. Chinese use almost any vegetable or combination of them in such a dish and you'll encounter this in restaurants as a complimentary appetizer, or you can find commercial variations of it in Asian food stores in glass jars.

Since the advent of the kimchiburger, it has become one of my favorite treatments of the American backyard burger. Simply spread a bit of butter and/or mayonnaise on the bun, add the cooked meat patty and cover the patty with a thick juicy spoon of *kimchi*. Or, if you enjoy a hot dog with sauerkraut, try using a hearty helping of *kimchi* instead.

Son Mitchell, whose time in Asia included a year in Korea, says you cannot use too much garlic in this recipe, but Mitchell says that about almost all Asian dishes. . . .

KIMCHI

Ingredients

1 small napa cabbage, 1½ to 2 pounds, 1 inch trimmed off the bottom, leaves separated and torn into 2 to 5 pieces, rinsed

3 tablespoons non-iodized pickling salt

2 spring onions, with roots and top few inches of green tops trimmed off and discarded, rinsed and quartered

3 inches of fresh ginger, peeled and sliced into ¼-inch coins

6 medium garlic cloves, peeled and lightly chopped

1 tablespoon sugar, or to taste

7 inches of long white radish, peeled, rinsed and sliced into ¼-inch coins and julienned

1½ tablespoons Korean powdered red pepper or substitute 2 fresh red Thai chilies cut in half lengthwise along with up to ½ teaspoon crushed red pepper flakes, or to taste

In a gallon plastic sealable freezer bag, add torn cabbage leaves, mixing well by hand with the salt. Seal bag and set aside 6 hours at room temperature, occasionally agitating bag vigorously. Cabbage will soften and reduce to about ¼ of its original volume. Drain and discard juice from bag and add cold tap water to come up about halfway on the cabbage. Agitate bag briefly and immediately drain juice from bag. Again add cold tap water about halfway up on the cabbage. Agitate bag briefly and immediately drain again, squeezing excess water out of cabbage. Place cabbage in a colander to drain for a half hour, retaining the bag. In a large bowl, mix onions, ginger, garlic, sugar, radish, powdered red pepper and blend together well, adding cabbage a little at a time and mixing thoroughly by hand. Return all ingredients to plastic bag, seal well, agitate bag and set aside at room temperature. Agitate bag from time to time over the next

2 to 3 days, after which the *kimchi* will be ready. It may then be refrigerated for several weeks in a stoneware or glass container, covered with clear plastic wrap, secured with a rubber band.

Tips—The amount of time you allow *kimchi* to work at room temperature is pretty much up to you, depending on the texture and maturity you want. Korean recipes tend to be vague on this point, ending with something like, "put the mixture in a crock" or "mix well and allow to stand." Over the years I've worked my way back from my earlier 10 to 15 day ferment and have finally settled on just 3 days. Discard it in the unlikely event mold forms on the top, a turn of events I've not encountered in nearly 40 years of sloshing this stuff around. Until you become accustomed to making *kimchi* you may find a batch too salty or too hot for you. If so, just dilute it with a little cold water. Use the long white radish shaped somewhat like a huge carrot which the Japanese call *daikon*. Round red radishes have not proven to be a great substitute for daikon in this recipe. Look for Korean powdered red *kimchi* pepper in Korean markets, in a clear plastic bag. The amount of garlic and red pepper powder may be varied to suit your taste. I use a little more than is indicated here as I prefer *kimchi* which carries itself with a bit of a swagger. Despite anything you may hear about its reputed long shelf-life, it's unlikely any *kimchi* could possibly outlast the refrigerator itself, no matter how much garlic and red pepper you use. Feel free to add a dash or so of paprika, if you'd like to enhance its red tint. Thai chili, short and thin and red or green, has a slight curve rather like a lady's little finger at tea.

Westerners Really Like these Eggs

Writings from the Han period, around 200 BC, list eggs as one of the common food items. But eggs surely have been an important part of the diet since Chinese began climbing trees and mucking through marshy duck terrain in search of a snack. How is it then, aside from egg fu yung or specks of yolk in fried rice, foreigners don't much associate eggs with Chinese cuisine? The eggs of chicken, duck, quail and pigeon are all widely popular with Chinese.

This Western perception likely stems from the fact relatively few foreigners have been able to experience a more full spectrum of Chinese food, such as a typical Chinese breakfast for example, where hard-boiled duck or chicken eggs are standard fare. Why not our ubiquitous Western sunny-side-up fried eggs? Likely it's because round-bottomed woks are less than ideally suited for frying an egg flat. The newer flat-bottomed woks work fine but that poses the question, how would you eat a sunny-side up egg with chopsticks?

The Chinese do dabble in a flat fried egg, cooked in a wok in a shallow pool of oil. But somehow, with a crispy white, it doesn't come across all that appealing to the uninitiated at dawn.

Traditionally, eggs are mixed until smooth and then swirled around in a lightly oiled wok, with the wok being tipped from side to side to create a thin skin which may be lifted out and used as a wrapper. This type of wrapper, or one made from flour, appears in a number of forms under a variety of names around the China Seas with different fillings rather like an egg roll or spring roll.

The differences between the egg roll and the spring roll are legion but folks tend to disagree on the exact details. It seems to more or less come down to whether the item is enrobed in a thin wheat or rice wrapper. Or whether it is fried or not. Or whether it contains meat. Well, something along those lines. The person taking your order never much seems to care what you call it. And whether you order egg rolls or spring rolls you will probably receive pretty much what you had in mind and you will enjoy it. If you want it with meat, just say so.

For the record, there is another popular egg roll in the Chinese lexicon. It is a sweet, crisp, rolled wafer, looking a bit like a hollow pastry cigar. You are unlikely to come across it in any Chinese restaurant. However, you may find them in a large Asian market along with the tinned cookies. A thinner version may be found in your own supermarket cookie section in a tin container, labeled "rolled wafers." These would serve well as dessert for a Chinese dinner at home, along with a small bowl of ice cream for dipping them into.

One of the more curious forms which eggs take in China is the appetizer known variously as the 1,000-year egg, 100-year egg, century egg or Ming Dynasty egg. Looking as if it might have come out of an archaeological dig, this actually involves an ancient preservation technique, coating duck or chicken eggs with lime, salt and ground charcoal and burying them for about 100 days. The black, jelly-like appearance and strong flavor will perhaps always remain something of a befuddlement to most Westerners.

It wasn't until the spiffy international hotels began appearing in China in the mid-1980s that the West's sunny-side-up egg became more common around the country.

Typically, breakfast buffets in these new five-star establishments were about the same as you would find in New York or San Francisco. Western tourists took this pretty much for granted, but the Old China Hands were really impressed, after years of breakfast peanuts, pickles, hard-boiled duck eggs and such.

The Western touches of the international hotels were eventually noted by some of the older Chinese hotels such as Shanghai's proud old Jin Jiang where the historic Shanghai Communiqué was signed by President Nixon and Premier Chou En-lai.

Built in 1931 as an elegant hostelry to serve Shanghai's chic French quarter, the top floor was for decades one of the more opulent public places to eat along the China Coast. The old dining room retained the aura of an earlier, less hurried time when it took weeks to get a letter to San Francisco. Thus it was a pleasant surprise when the hotel instituted a Western breakfast buffet on the top floor. Eagerly checking it out on my next visit, I found it not memorable. But not all that bad. Except for the fried eggs. They were stone cold. The cook had found it more convenient to fry up the whole shebang all at once before the dining room opened. Like maybe the evening before.

The head waiter paused at my table to ask how I'd found the buffet.

"Quite good. Except the eggs are cold."

"But Westerners like cold fried eggs."

"Really?"

The next morning the head waiter paused at my table, nodded brightly toward the other guests and said, "See, everyone is eating cold fried eggs."

That's not to say you can't get a good cold egg in China.

There's an easy and interesting cold egg appetizer foreigners really do enjoy which adds an artistic touch to the table and is an excellent conversation piece as guests invariably ask how on earth you give the peeled egg a marbled appearance. . . .

MARBLED TEA EGGS
Ingredients
4 eggs

½ tablespoon salt

1 tablespoon dark soy sauce

1 tablespoon regular soy sauce

1 tablespoon black tea or 2 tea bags

1 tablespoon five spice powder

2 whole star anise or 16 broken points

1 cinnamon stick, 2 inches long

Accompaniment
roasted pepper salt (page 248)

Place eggs in a single layer in pan and cover in cold water 1 inch over tops. Bring to boil over high heat. Reduce to low. Cook 20 minutes. Place in ice water to cool, for easier peeling later. When cool enough to handle, with the back of a teaspoon very gently crack (but not remove) the shells with a bit of a cobweb pattern of fine cracks around the side of the egg leaving the top and bottom relatively intact. Without yet adding eggs, in a saucepan small enough to hold eggs fairly snugly (to concentrate the infusion) mix well together salt, dark and regular soy sauce, tea, five spice powder, star anise and cinnamon. Estimating, add enough cold water to just cover eggs. Bring to a low simmer, stirring occasionally. Add eggs, cover and reduce heat to lowest setting for 30 minutes, occasionally turning eggs gently with a spoon for even coloring. Add additional hot water as required to keep liquid level just above the eggs. After the half-hour simmer, turn off heat and leave eggs in infusion to cool to room temperature, turning occasionally. Place saucepan with infusion and eggs in the refrigerator for at least 24 hours, turning eggs from time to time to color and flavor evenly. Remove eggs, discarding infusion. Carefully remove shells and any membrane under cold running water, revealing marbling. Pat dry with paper towel. Serve whole, halved or quartered, either chilled or at room temperature, on a serving plate as an appetizer alongside a small dish of roasted pepper salt. Or serve in a small dish on a bed of roasted pepper salt, perhaps along with some hard-boiled quail eggs if you wish. Marbled tea eggs also may be used to garnish other dishes.

Tips—Tap the eggs gently to create delicate cracks. Whacking away too vigorously can result in eggs with Rorschach blots of rampaging rhinos and squashed bugs, rather than a subtle marbled effect. If you can eat peeled hard-boiled eggs with chopsticks it's OK to feel a little smug about it. The trick is to hold the egg with a gossamer-light grip so it doesn't become a projectile. Or, hold your chopsticks stationary and parallel to cradle the egg rather than trying to pincer it. It's a good idea to provide spoons as a safety net when serving particularly slippery food with chopsticks. Older eggs peel easier so you may consider holding eggs for a week or so in the refrigerator before using. This recipe works equally well with just two eggs. Leaving these eggs in the infusion in the refrigerator for at least 24 hours affords a deeper marbled coloring.

*   *   *   *

Petite and speckled, quail eggs add another nice touch to the cuisine of the China Seas. Basically, cooking quail eggs comes down to two choices, either poaching or hard boiling. They can be fried as a fun food for youngsters, though dealing with all those little fried eggs isn't much fun for the cook.

POACHED QUAIL EGGS

To poach quail eggs, use your regular poacher with a light film of butter, as you would if you were doing chicken eggs, reducing the poaching time to about a minute or two until the white is done. You can also do this in a steamer, opening eggs into buttered soy sauce dishes. Cracking raw eggs this small and getting the yolk out intact calls for a bit more care and you may find this easier if you carefully snip part way around the shell at its midpoint with a pair of sharp-pointed scissors, such as the type used in manicuring or sewing. When the whites are done, remove poacher from the heat and, with a wide soup spoon, gently ease eggs out of the poacher and add them to a clear soup or use as a garnish for a variety of stir-fried dishes.

HARD-BOILED QUAIL EGGS

To hard boil quail eggs, before adding eggs, fill saucepan with enough water to cover eggs. Chinese say that quail eggs peel easier if you add a pinch of salt and four drops of vinegar to the water. Bring water to a boil, reduce heat to a simmer and with eggs at room temperature, gently add them to the water and continue simmering 5 or 6 minutes. Set aside with eggs still in the hot water for another 5 minutes. Carefully remove eggs and plunge them into ice water for easier peeling. When cool enough to handle, roll each egg gently back and forth between the fingers of both hands to fracture shell as completely as possible and carefully peel eggs under cold running water. You can accomplish a higher level of fracturing by also agitating the eggs vigorously in a lidded pan. Peel from the large end of the egg, and rub off any clinging membrane and pat dry with a paper towel.

Tips—Before cooking quail eggs, check for freshness by placing them in a bowl of water. Fresh eggs lay on the bottom. Older eggs stand on end and may bob up and down a bit. That's OK but a floating egg is past its prime and should be discarded. When hard boiling, remember older eggs peel easier than fresh ones, so if they do well on the float test you may want to hold them a week or two as quail eggs are a bit more difficult to peel than regular eggs. As you might expect, you are more likely to find fresher quail eggs in a large busy market than in a little Mom and Pop outlet where there is a slower turnover. Ask whether they know when the eggs came in, to lessen the likelihood of floaters. And discard any which may be cracked.

A small bowl of peeled hard-boiled quail eggs may be served as appetizers. But remember, in the company of chopsticks, peeled hard-boiled quail eggs are among the most aerodynamic of foods. It's in their DNA to fly. It's possible to pick them up with chopsticks held parallel and stationary, cradling rather than pincering the egg. But to prevent their being lobbed across the table like an unruly backhand, you'll find a small spoon is more user-friendly. These eggs also may be served as a garnish for a variety of compatible dishes or, either whole or cut in two, they may be used to enhance a clear soup. The rule is, if you think they will work with a dish they probably will. Use them with sprigs of fresh coriander leaves to brighten the edge around a platter of chicken, or whatever. Or serve two in a porcelain Chinese soup spoon on a bed of roasted pepper salt as a side dish.

*   *   *   *

While salt and pepper shakers are not something you find on traditional Chinese tables, the Chinese have come up with a delightful salt and pepper variation which Westerners invariably enjoy and almost always ask, "What is this?" And that's not inflected with trepidation, but in a tone which suggests the next question will be, "How do you make it?" It's an excellent and highly flavorful condiment into which guests may dip eggs, poultry, fried and oily foods and just about anything which responds to the application of a little spice. It affords an assertive burst of flavor so use it sparingly.

Here's the answer to the question about how it's made. . . .

ROASTED PEPPER SALT
Ingredients

1 tablespoon Sichuan peppercorns
3 tablespoons salt

In a dry frying pan over moderate heat, roast peppercorns and salt together, stirring frequently with a wooden spoon until you smell the roasting peppercorns and the salt begins to take on a slightly darker color, about 6 minutes. Peppercorns may smoke a little but should not be allowed to scorch. Remove from pan and allow to cool on a dish. Grind down well with a mortar and pestle and strain through a fine sieve, discarding the remaining bits of peppercorn husks. Place on the table in condiment—or small soy sauce—dishes at each diner's place.

Tips—Sichuan peppercorns, not strictly a true pepper but rather the seed of the prickly ash tree, are available in Asian food stores. In a sealed jar, roasted pepper salt keeps for months at room temperature in a dry, dark place.

Been There, Ate That

A Chinese sage once observed, "A journey of 1,000 miles is more enlightening than a year of study." Well, maybe. That would seem to depend largely on where you're traveling or what you're studying. But there's no denying that if you pay attention and maintain an open mind while traveling around the China Seas, it's possible to learn something new every day; something which will come in handy somewhere along the line. Particularly when it comes to food.

You are virtually assured of being quickly accepted into another culture if you have a genuine interest in the food, enjoy it, and perhaps even learn to properly pronounce its name, how to shop for it and how to cook it.

When the Great Depression hit I was just one year old, so I had no idea anything unusual was going on. In those days children learned to eat what was on their plate without running a critique on it with the cook.

It was good, and made meal planning easier, to see our youngsters taking on our spirit of confidence and curiosity toward unfamiliar dishes. Not counting that one lapse when little Heather, Heidi and Lesli mutually and vigorously instituted a boycott of ham sandwiches upon figuring out that they were derived from cuddly pink piglets.

In later years I came to appreciate that learning to eat everything on your plate and developing a spirit of adventure about it has its benefits. Chatting at an embassy reception in Manila with a stranger, I mentioned having recently returned from a trip into northwest Thailand, which sparked his interest as he said he knew that part of the country well. Really? Yes. He'd survived World War II as a prisoner of the Japanese on the River Kwai. Wow.

Fortunately, I hadn't complained about what a rough trip I'd had, although I had in fact, in a remote jungle village, contracted, concurrently, hepatitis and dysentery, a combination which results in the mere sight and smell of food making one nauseous. Finally, to kill what was killing me, the doctor prescribed arsenic, which rates quite high on the list of curiosities I've ingested over the years.

What, I asked the River Kwai veteran, had perhaps contributed most to him not being one of the 13,000 Allied prisoners who died building the "Death Railway" through the jungle for the Emperor? A trait common among survivors, he said, aside from having a buddy you could count on in a pinch, was, "We would eat orange peels and things others wouldn't eat." Indeed, military survival training today covers the dietary advantages of snakes and bugs, making the point that protein comes in forms other than hamburgers and that eating something with some nutrition can be better than eating nothing.

Having eaten, and usually relished, just about everything which has ever been chased, caught, cleaned and cooked in that part of the world, it does present something of a challenge when asked what was the most memorable. Well, maybe sautéed caterpillars. But later I would recall the fried scorpions. Or those cobras we had for lunch in the hills of Guangdong. Or exchanging toasts with raw turtle blood.

Historically, this all stems from two distinct culinary scenarios which emerged over the millennia. On the one hand there's simple peasant fare, the source of many of our greatest dishes; often inspired by nothing more than necessity. Then we have imperial fare, with palace cooks coming up with all manner of the most rare ingredients and often outlandish innovations to impress the boss.

My first visit to Tokyo in January 1964 was simply a stopover for a few days on the way to the new job promoting US wheat sales to Asia's rice eaters. And here at a reception on the first evening in town was an unexpected touch of home. A bright little blob of orange salmon eggs, just like the ones we'd used as bait in the Alpine streams of NE Oregon's high country.

This was long before *sushi* bars became popular in the US and I'd never before encountered salmon eggs as an appetizer, nestled on a tiny slice of toast. Discovering how flavorful they were was a pleasant surprise, that "first step" into the "journey of 1,000 miles" discovering delightful dishes which back home were considered bait, animal feed, or something to be chopped off and cast aside.

Initial exploratory probes into open-air markets in Hong Kong did raise some eyebrows, along with questions as to how on earth one could equate those sights and smells with something good to eat. But if you're lucky enough to have the opportunity to have the time to stick with it, in no time at all these sights and smells will be whetting your appetite.

Then there's Taipei's Snake Alley where you find a lot of skewered, barbecued stuff which looks suspiciously like something out of the Jurassic Period. All very tasty and well prepared. But different. And almost certain to set an environmentalist's teeth on edge.

So it came to pass one morning in Hong Kong that I persuaded a visiting group of wheat farmers from our board of directors to forego the hotel's coffee shop for a *dim sum* breakfast across the street. Arriving at the crowded, colorful and cacophonous restaurant, I explained that while they were accustomed to a formidable farm breakfast back home—typically something like three eggs, fried potatoes, bacon, sausage, toast, juice and coffee—this experience would afford insights into the challenge we faced in trying to wean the Cantonese away from this two-hour breakfast—with a pet caged bird and the morning paper on the table—and, instead, have toast or a sweet bun on the run.

I motioned to the waitress that we'd take whatever special item she was hawking from her food cart. A spicy cloud swirled from the bamboo steamer as she lifted the lid. All five board members leaned forward and peered apprehensively into the little steamer.

Yummy little meat balls?

Sweet and succulent shrimp in a gossamer rice flour wrapper?

No.

Fortune had somehow chosen to cast before us the star of any respectable *dim sum* menu. The favored delicacy known as "claws of the phoenix." Chicken feet. Hmmmm.

The board member from Idaho said, "We get the idea. Now can we go back to the hotel for a real breakfast?"

Well, of course.

The *Dim Sum* Incident was followed a year later with the Parable of the Pigeon. This occurred in Shatin, in Hong Kong's northern New Territories. Today, Shatin is a bustling, modern satellite city but in those days it was little more than a quiet crossroads alongside a tidal flat. Snuggled in the shade of rich green hills, alongside the tracks of the old Kowloon-Canton Railway, was an unassuming little restaurant which was widely renowned for its pigeon dishes. With the sprawling skyscraper urbanization, the restaurant became so difficult to find that the last time I took visitors up that way we ended up having pizza in a shopping mall instead.

In the old days I often took American visitors to the pigeon restaurant for a cultural experience as part of a Sunday outing. On one of these occasions, a member of the group confided later that while he'd found the pigeon delicious, he'd had a little trouble working up the gumption to take the first bite. The floppy little head on the cooked bird had put him off.

On the next visit with a batch of first-timers, I took the precaution of quietly instructing the waiter that we wanted a platter of pigeons. Without heads. However, when the dish was brought to the table, the heads were still attached.

As I speculated on how best to salvage the situation, the waiter suddenly flourished a pair of scissors which he plunged down, in a great glittering arc, snapping across the platter as if pruning a hedge. Clickety-snip-click-clack! Pigeon heads bounced across the table in all directions like brown, beaked ping pong balls.

You can be sure our waiter, on returning home that evening, said to his wife, "Honey, you can't guess the weird way this American asked me to serve pigeon."

After having undertaken this dish at home a few times, I got to wondering, how might a little Rock Cornish game hen from the supermarket respond to this recipe? Happily, with the only adjustment being an additional 20 minutes in the steamer, the Cornish hen responded beautifully.

The Lovely Charlene, something of an authority on both high and low Asian cuisine, enthusiastically rates my "Cantonese" Cornish hen as "outstanding" and she prefers it to the pigeon. . . .

ROAST PIGEON
serves 2

Ingredients

2 spring onions, rinsed, with roots and top few inches of green tops trimmed off and discarded, finely chopped

1-inch piece of fresh ginger, peeled and finely chopped

⅛ cup regular soy sauce

1 tablespoon Shao Xing wine or good dry sherry

2 tablespoons honey

2 medium garlic cloves, peeled, finely chopped or passed through a garlic press

½ teaspoon five spice powder

¼ teaspoon freshly ground black pepper

1 squab, about 1 pound, giblets removed

4 cups peanut oil for frying

Garnish
5 sprigs of fresh rinsed coriander leaves or watercress
Accompaniment
roasted pepper salt (page 248)

Place onions and ginger in a mortar and grind into a paste. In small saucepan mix paste with soy sauce, wine, honey, garlic, five spice powder, pepper and ¼ cup of cold water. Stir and bring marinade to low boil. Immediately remove from heat and set aside 10 minutes to cool. Place squab in a bowl or pan or sealable plastic bag and pour marinade into and over it. Marinate squab 2 hours in the refrigerator, turning occasionally and spooning marinade into and over squab. Drain squab and discard marinade. Place squab in steamer, cover and steam over low boiling water 25 minutes. (If doing Cornish hen instead, steam a total of about 45 minutes.) To check for doneness, if juices run clear from a test slice into the leg joint it is ready. Remove squab and when cool enough to handle pat squab dry with paper towels. With kitchen shears, cut squab in half lengthwise. Then cut crosswise to quarter squab, with each piece having either a wing or a leg. (Optionally, cut off head.) Warm wok over medium high heat about 2 minutes. Add oil and increase heat to high and when oil begins to shimmer and light haze (not smoke) begins to rise, add two pieces of squab, maintaining a constant high heat. When pieces begin to turn a golden ruby brown on the underside, about 1½ minutes, turn once and brown other side about 1 minute. Drain on paper towels. Repeat with other 2 pieces of squab. Serve hot with garnish around the rim of the serving place along with a side dish of roasted pepper salt.

Tip—The oil is hot enough when tiny bubbles will rise around the end of a wooden chopstick inserted into it.

Best Food in the World

Humility is one of the most charming and indelible of all the great virtues of the Chinese. Except when it comes to their cuisine. Then humility goes the way of foot binding.

Chinese cuisine has influenced the cooking of the entire Southeast Asian region, whether it be Thailand, Indonesia or wherever. And while it is acclaimed internationally as one of the best cuisines in the world, the Chinese see it simply as *the* best.

One evening at dinner in Guangzhou just north of Hong Kong, a friend of many years, Peng Qi Fu, didn't bat an eye at my conceding that while Chinese cuisine is outstanding, people's feelings toward food are essentially a reflection of what mother used to make.

"You're Chinese so you think that's best. The French think French food is best and Eskimos probably dream of polar bear soup and seal stew on cold winter nights."

Pondering that—with chopsticks frozen for a moment in mid-trajectory—Peng replied, "But, there are more Chinese than anybody else and they say Chinese food is best. So if most people say Chinese food is best, well, it's best."

Peng's logic isn't unique. A typical endorsement surfaced in a letter from Old China Hand Larry Senger, Agricultural Counselor at the US Embassy in Beijing. In the early 1980s, we covered many rural and urban nooks and crannies between Shanghai and Hong Kong. Often with Peng, in his role as a leader in the food industry. Larry wrote, "Each time I go to a restaurant here in Beijing I discover another extraordinary dish I've never had before. And I've lived here two and a half years, in Guangzhou for three and in Taipei for two, a total of nearly eight years in China. The variety of food in China is endless, delicious and totally beyond the scope of Western cuisine. It's the best food in the world."

It brings to mind a Chinese delegation I'd escorted to the United States a few years earlier. Dining at one of the more popular restaurants in San Francisco's Chinatown, a young lady in our group remarked, "Looking around at the customers here you can really see how much better Chinese food is for you. Many Americans are really overweight, but the people eating here are very trim because they eat healthy Chinese food."

Chinese cuisine—off the heady, heavy, death-by-duck banquet circuit—indeed affords a healthy diet if one sticks with the more simple staples. But this wasn't the case here. I pointed out that many of the diners were speaking European languages. Few were using chopsticks and they all were indulging in rich, fatty, battered, banquet-style dishes, evidence of their being tourists enjoying a night out in one of the world's zingiest Chinatowns.

Of course—in deference to the ramifications of face—my comment was immediately tempered by noting that, on the other hand, I'm not overweight "and I do eat a lot of Chinese food and it is well-known that Chinese cuisine is loaded with things that are good for you." My testimonial spawned knowing nods and broad smiles, affirming their faith in the clear superiority of the Chinese kitchen.

In seven decades of exposure to Chinese food, one of the most startling endorsements of it I ever heard came up one morning at breakfast with Stanley Rittenberg, author of *The Man Who Stayed Behind*, the riveting account of his 30 years in China. The book jacket reads, "In 1946, a young American marched with the Revolutionaries across war-torn China. Over the next three decades he remained to fight their fights, keep their secrets, and befriend their leaders.

He was invited into their inner circles of power, and survived 16 years in their prisons. Now he has returned to tell his story."

Heavy stuff.

"So," he asked as we sat down, "how's that cookbook coming along?"

"It's like that journey of 1,000 miles. One step at a time, as the Chinese say."

"Wonderful. Just wonderful." And then, this man who had marched with Mao, endured China's prisons and survived World War II in China, the Civil War, the Cultural Revolution and everything in between, said, "Looking back, all those years, the thing that stands out in my mind is—the food."

That's pretty heavy stuff too. But that's how Chinese cuisine is, to those who really get to know it and appreciate its variety.

Jack Kerouac, the scribe prince of the Beat Generation, was among the fortunate. In a reminiscence of the old San Francisco Chinatown I roamed and knew well in my youth, Kerouac would later write:

"I sit in the Chinatown park on a dark bench and take the air, drinking in the sight of the foody delicious neons of my restaurant blinking in the little street . . . Then I go in my restaurant, order from the Chinese menu, and instantly they bring me smoked fish, curried chicken, fabulous duck cakes, unbelievably delicious . . . ah I eat—and eat—till midnight. . . ."

In the West we tend to turn up our nose at a number of really wonderful, nutritious and tasty things which are popular in Asia and which, in prehistoric days, were surely staples on which our earliest ancestors survived. Today, we don't think of them as food. Or we're unaware of them. Or wouldn't know where to find them or how to prepare them if we were so inclined. Or we consider them too exotic. Or better directed into animal feed channels.

Pea tendrils, the tender tips, leaves and stems of the young pea plant, are a classic example. Stir-fried in peanut oil with chunks of fresh crab, minced onion and garlic, they provide a delicious, nutritious, quick and easy side dish or main course. We happened upon this decades ago in an obscure little eatery in the course of an outing in Taichung, south of Taipei. And it remains a family favorite. It's unlikely you'll come across this on a menu outside Asia. Or, even find it in any other Asian cookbook. But it is seasonally available in the produce section of well-stocked Asian markets outside Asia. Chinese friends call it the evergreen vegetable, as, when hothouse grown, it can be available throughout the year. You may perhaps be able to special order it in advance at a nearby Chinese restaurant.

So don't be surprised if Westerners soon discover this great dish. . . .

PEA TENDRILS WITH CRAB MEAT
serves 2 to 4
Ingredients
1 pound fresh pea tendrils
7 tablespoons peanut oil
½ teaspoon salt
1 tablespoon round white or yellow onion, finely minced
2 medium garlic cloves, peeled, finely minced or passed through a garlic press
1 cup fresh cooked Dungeness crab meat

Trim tendrils into shorter stems about 5 or 6 inches long and discard any less-tender bottoms. Soak the retained tendrils 5 to 10 minutes in a pot of cold water. Drain and shake off as much water as possible. Place in colander and set aside 5 to 10 minutes to drain. Remove from colander and shake water from tendrils again and place on paper towels for a few minutes to drain further. Warm your largest wok over medium high heat about 2 minutes. Add peanut oil to wok. Increase heat to high and add salt for flavoring as well as to somewhat reduce the hot oil's splattering when the wet tendrils are added. When oil shimmers and light haze (not smoke) begins to rise, immediately add tendrils and stir together with the onion, garlic and crab meat. Over high heat stir-fry continually with long wooden cooking chopsticks or a wooden spatula, stirring ingredients 6 or 7 minutes until well mixed. Tendrils will be reduced to about $1/3$ their original volume and will take on a shiny dark green color with the look of cooked spinach. Immediately turn out onto a serving bowl or plate and serve hot.

Tips—This may be made without crab, or with two or three large raw shrimp, peeled and chopped. Pea tendrils are found in the produce section of Asian food stores. Look for them when fresh peas appear in the market. There is the large-leaf and a small-leaf variety, the latter having flat, smooth, pale green leaves, circular in shape and about the size of a fingernail. The large-leaf variety, with leaves about the size of sweet basil leaves, is favored for this recipe as it affords more surface area, to better carry the flavor of the ingredients. If you have trouble finding pea tendrils, ask when they may be available. They should have a fresh crisp appearance. Always take care when adding wet ingredients to hot oil as the water will cause a momentary splatter. Canned crab, depending on the brand, can be disappointing in texture and flavor so fresh cooked crab is recommended for this dish.

After Words

Fairly early, I realized if I wanted to be able to always enjoy the dishes I was coming across in the China Seas I had best start learning how to prepare them. That seemed easy enough. I'd clattered about in kitchens and markets since my early teens in San Francisco, just minutes from Chinatown. I moved on, and spent half my life experiencing wonderful food and rather surprising edible cultural curiosities in more far-away places with strange sounding names than I ever imagined back when I was a knobby-kneed kid looking out across the Pacific, wondering who and what the heck might be on the other side. Discovering the answer to that has proved a grand adventure.

I found myself drawing energy and enthusiasm from the challenges and opportunities which awaited Asia's untried foreign intruders in those last decades of the 20th century. These were historic times, as Old China emerged from generations of isolation to become a major player on the world stage. Along with that, we shared with Hong Kong its final 30 years as the crown jewel of the British Empire. Great friends and good luck loaded the dice in our favor. Such as that afternoon Chinese government associates insisted on taking me out of my hotel, a couple blocks from Tiananmen Square "for our invitation you cannot refuse, to overnight at an ancient temple on the outskirts of Beijing." Despite my protests I went along. Within a few hours, soldiers would begin clearing out the student occupiers from Tiananmen.

Through it all, my work around Asia with US Wheat Associates, in cooperation with the Foreign Agricultural Service of the US Department of

Agriculture and Asian third-party business interests, contributed to the modernization and expansion of the Asian food industry. New quality products were popularized, bringing about better nutrition and more varied diets. We were a small band of food revolutionaries and foreign governments embraced us. Everyone benefitted through the entire economic pipeline from our wheat fields to the Asian consumers. Countless jobs and peripheral economic support activities blossomed, on both sides of the Pacific. Swept along by the power of mutuality, Asia benefitted through our many technological transfers, training programs and related support activities, while the US economy benefitted through the return of billions of dollars in cash wheat sales over the years.

My shot at seeing if fortune cookies (a wheat product) could be popularized in China got nowhere, as I expected. But the Chinese got a kick out of seeing how to make them.

Our family's Asian adventure, followed by 13 years of semi-retirement on the Oregon Coast, followed by relocating to Wilsonville on the rural fringe of Portland afforded us a wonderfully memorable life experience.

Summing up, it confirmed for us—A good life, like good fried rice, does indeed have a lot to do with how much good stuff you are willing to stir into it.

EXPLORE ASIA WITH BLACKSMITH BOOKS

From retailers around the world or from *www.blacksmithbooks.com*